IN THE

ROMANTIC

STYLE

IN THE ROMANTIC STYLE

CREATING INTIMACY, FANTASY AND CHARM IN THE CONTEMPORARY HOME

by Linda Chase and Laura Cerwinske

Thames & Hudson

CONTENTS

Text copyright © 1990 by Laura Cerwinske and Linda Chase

First published in hardcover in the United States of America in 1990 by
Thames & Hudson Inc., 500 Fifth Avenue, New York, New York 10110

First published in hardcover in the United Kingdom in 1990 by
Thames & Hudson Ltd, 181A High Holborn, London WC1V 7QX

First paperback edition 2000

Library of Congress Catalog Card Number 98-60337

ISBN 0-500-28244-7

British Library Cataloguing-in-Publication Data
A catalogue record for this book is available from the British Library

Designed by Zimmering, Zinn and Madison

Printed and bound in Malaysia by Times Publishing

Acknowledgments

Our gratitude to Ralph Levy, certified member and past president of the Appraisers Association of America and teacher and lecturer at Hofstra University, for his generous gift of time and knowledge; to Max Drazen for his constant support, sense of humor, and late-night calls; to Sarah Poole for her dedication and valuable assistance; to Carol Wagner and Michael McManus for their loving hospitality and outrageous phone bill; to Thomas Kornay for the adventure; and to David Goman and the many others who contributed their efforts to the accomplishment of this book: Karin Linder, Linwood E. Cutler, Charles Berendt, Bill Biniasz, Eddie Hamby, Ingrid Henderson, Julio Martinez, Yves Bolognino, Henner Tayir, Steven Joseph, Alan Palmer, Monique de Warren, Roger Cantrell, Rusty Risbrough, Troy Webb, Floyd Ackles, Lucy Angulo, Vito D'Alessandro, Lois Rosenthal, Wayne Pollard, Irma Densen, Iraj Noorollah, Roger Bettle, Patrick Cordes, Larry Berman, Rafi Ghodsian, Steven Moser, Alain-Paul Sevilla, Michael Bowers, Lenna Tyler-Kast, Michael Kane, Roger Vlitos, Linda Tan, Carla Pellerano Walker, Sylvia Wood, Marsha Coppes, Luis Palacio, Augusto Petruschansky and Caroline Northcoat Sidnam.

We also wish to acknowledge all the designers and photographers whose work comprises this book, with special thanks to David Phelps, a dedicated photographer and a *patient* one, and to Janet Doyle whose steady guidance kept us on course and whose light touch elegantly enhanced our thoughts.

$\mathcal{I}$NTRODUCTION

The room is not only the beginning of architecture, it is an extension of the self....The large room and the small room, the tall room and the low room, the room with the fireplace and the room without, all become great events in your mind.

—Louis Kahn
Between Silence and Light

WHETHER THEY ARE A REVERIE of sweet disorder or an elaborate staging of domestic theater, rooms decorated in the romantic style reflect a sheer exuberance for life. Timeless and inviting, they are distinguished by elegance, abundance, beauty, grace, and a frank indulgence in the pleasures of the world. Seductive refuges from the cold intellectualism of modernism and the stark geometries of post-modernism, they are created out of the desire to compose a place where those we love will be comfortable. Always evolving and never finished, they pay homage to courtship and frame the dreams of the soul. They are, in the words of the twelfth-century troubadours, sanctuaries filled with "what the eyes have made welcome to the heart."

The romantic style ranges from the whimsically enchanted to the voluptuously undecorated. Warmly lit and dressed in beautiful fabrics, romantic rooms soothe the spirit and tantalize the eye. Abundantly furnished with *canapés*, settees, overstuffed chairs, plush cushions, rugs, and tapestries, they beckon with the promise of comfort. Cluttered with keepsakes, they lead, like a maze, through interiors where not all is revealed at once. Highly personal and without regard for convention, they celebrate spontaneity.

Rooms designed by Linda Chase, the co-author of this book, often reflect her passion for the fashions of eighteenth-century Europe. In France, in particular, everything from court attire to drapery and upholstery was embellished with poufs, flounces, tassels, and pendants, and Miss Chase's interiors frequently display these romantic flourishes. She is also drawn to the rich pinks, corals, aubergines, celadon greens, and French blues that appear often in Aubusson tapestry, and to the bleeding tones of Indian fabrics. In her Los Angeles home, a charming but originally colorless hillside bungalow built in the 1920s, she used these hues, as well as

The Los Angeles living room of Linda Chase

terra-cotta and the warm ochers found throughout Europe, to revive the house's personality. "I felt I'd discovered a secret, a treasure from Hollywood's golden years, a faded star in need of new life," she says. "Restoring it was like applying fresh *maquillage* to the face of a forgotten diva."

Her New York *pied-à-terre*, located in a modern apartment building, was totally devoid of any architectural character and called for more dramatic measures. Miss Chase softened the rooms' hard edges and unforgiving corners with generous swags of linen and antique lace. She brought the stark, newly-constructed interior walls to life with Italianate floral designs subtly hand-painted over several coats of a deep parchment glaze. She replaced the apartment's standard contemporary light fixtures with antique wall sconces and lightened the dark, dull parquet floors by hand-painting them a celadon green and pale ocher in a classic European country pattern.

When the architectural nature of a house or the temperament of a client calls for an approach altogether different from these, Linda Chase might create a romantic look by using a monochromatic palette, bold wood tones, or distressed metallics. All can similarly illustrate the sensuality, wit, playfulness, capriciousness, and poetry that express the romantic style. For, unrestricted by tradition and not limited to one historical period or a particular geography, romantic rooms draw upon many varied tastes and cultural influences. They can, for example, marry the femininity of Victorian fashion with the charm of country French or the glamour of Art Deco with the exoticism of the Orient and the Near East.

With its sultry climate and indolent customs, the Near East, in fact, has one of the world's longest traditions of romantic culture. Its fashion was unknown to the West, however, until the nineteenth century, when it came into vogue as a result, in part, of the published writings of the explorer Sir Richard Burton and the reports of archaeologists and other scholars who accompanied Napoleon's armies into Egypt. By the middle of the century, when tales of the Casbah and works of Asian literature, such as *The Rubaiyat of Omar Khayyam* and *A Thousand and One Nights* were translated, images of "tents strewn with carpets of every imaginable color," and "halls with walls of solid gold, the air of which was refreshed by fountains falling into basins of turquoise," began to spice escapists' dreams. From Turkey came descriptions of the Seraglio, at the heart of which were the harem and the apartments of the sultan and "the veiled crown," his mother. Labyrinthine walls and courtyards encircled this secret refuge, from which a warren of subterranean passages and stairways wound to treasure vaults and to the corridor of the baths, known as the golden path, down which the chosen *odalisque* was led to the monarch's bed. From terraces and pavilions set in tulip gardens, the sultan could look out at the distant vistas of the Bosporus and the mosques on the far Asiatic shore.

In Europe, interiors were taken to romantic extremes by such architects as William Burges, who spent twenty years working on a turreted and moated "summer house" called Castell Coch for the Lord of Bute, known in the nineteenth century as the wealthiest man in the world. The castle's medieval-looking interior is painted in bright reds, blues, greens, and golds. A dome over the living room rises forty feet, and is painted inside with the images of birds and butterflies in flight. Toward the apex, the species become birds and moths of the night and the background color changes from azure to indigo. A fireplace in the circular main room of the castle is big enough for several people to stand inside, yet Burges managed to keep the atmosphere cozy. When he designed the marquis' bed, he had it made of carved wood, painted scarlet and crowned by four large crystal balls on its posts. In the teacups he designed, leaves were strained through a setting of rubies.

Other excessive romantics include "Mad" King Ludwig of Bavaria, Wagner's patron, who built fanciful confections in stone where floors were wheeled away to reveal baths the size of swimming pools, and the czars of Imperial Russia who tucked follies, pavilions, and all manner of trysting places throughout the grounds of Pavlovsk, one of their imperial country palaces. These rendezvous spots, hidden in the dense woods and pine groves of the 600-acre estate, included a Chinese kiosk with an umbrella-shaped roof; a *charbonnière's* (charcoal burner's) hut with a saddle-shaped roof covered with earth and moss and fitted inside with a stately interior; a hermit's cell faced with tree bark and outfitted with specially made rustic furniture; and a Swiss chalet with a thatched roof and plain exterior that was lavishly furnished with everything from marquetry tables and brocade-upholstered chairs to embroidered linens and exquisite porcelains.

One of the most famous—and frivolous—of all the romantic follies created by royalty was, no doubt, Marie Antoinette's *laiterie*, a working dairy farm, built on the grounds of Versailles and modeled after a classical temple. Inside, a marble-floored atrium led onto a grotto surrounded by pools. From secret fountains, veils of water bathed a statue of Venus.

A more elevated shrine to the Muses was the salon of Madame de Rambouillet, a seventeenth-century woman of manners, letters, and grace. Only a half-light, suffused with muted silver, was allowed to enter the windows of her spacious apartment, known as the *salon bleu*. It was decorated with blue silken curtains, blue and gold upholstery, and great crystal vases filled with spring flowers made to bloom throughout the year. The *chambre* was also furnished with numerous screens to encourage intimate and confidential gatherings. In the innermost alcove she received her most honored guests, writers, artists, and courtesans with whom she conspired to draw up a new code of court behavior that encouraged the appreciation of beauty and language.

While rituals of pleasure consumed the eighteenth-century French, in Italy the excavations of Pompeii, Herculaneum, and the Temple of Paestum unearthed fresh visions of antiquity. European society, looking to the past to regenerate its sense of history, embraced the imagery of ruins. In his drawings of Rome, the engraver and academician Giovanni Battista Piranesi, who was passionately involved with the recovery of truths from the past and who regarded classical antiquity as a living world of experience and inspiration, created a mystical fantasy of classical times with vine-embellished depictions of crumbling Roman architecture. The English architects William Chambers and William Kent transposed this vision to the English landscape, where they created

gardens designed to look as if nature had scarcely been altered, in which replications of antique ruins were placed to add to their gardens' charm.

The idea of the garden as an extension of architecture has been a continuous theme throughout history. The Persians were known for fragrant courtyards whose beauty was judged by their ability to attract nightingales. The Alhambra's Court of the Lions, a closed-in garden composed around a carved stone fountain, planted with orange trees and aromatic herbs, and fashioned after the palm-set oases of the Arabian desert, was built as a symbol of paradise.

Architecture itself, in fact, reiterates nature, simulating earth and sky with floor and ceiling. Similarly, romantic interiors draw inspiration from the colors, textures, and shapes of the landscape. Soft pinks, gentle lavenders, and faded blues, like hollyhocks, suggest the sweetness of an English garden or the innocence of a first romantic encounter; classical greens, lily whites, and the blue of the sky recall the formality of French *parterres*; brown, golds, and harvest colors are evocative of autumn.

Colors also evoke the grandeur of history, royalty, and the stage: vivid reds and burnished golds herald the baroque; deep purples and indigo blues are regal; the brilliant palette of the Ballets Russes, which was brought to Paris in the 1920s by the Russian impresario Serge Diaghilev, exploded the visual concepts of the Edwardian era: As Diana Vreeland described it, "Red had never before been red and violet had never been violet. They were always slightly...grayed....[But with the Ballets Russes] colors became as sharp as a knife: red red, violent violet, and orange—when I say 'orange' I mean red orange, not yellow orange; jade green and cobalt blue. And the fabrics—the silks, the satins, and the brocades, embroidered with seed pearls and braid, shot with silver and gold and trimmed with fur and lace—were of an Oriental *splendeur*. There's never been such luxury since."

Whether you have just recently embraced the romantic style or are an avowed devotee, and whether you are seeking the opulence of a Russian ballroom or the simple charm of an English cottage, you will find this book an inspiring guide to extracting from your own life the material and imagination for adding intimacy and allure to your home. It will show you how to transform simple everyday objects into objects of desire and how, even without an aristocratic purse, it is possible to make romantic rooms out of majestic dreams.

Laura Cerwinske

*A dining room by
interior designer Diane Burn*

SURFACES AND FINISHES

We walked past the menservants into a hall with orange marble walls and a mauve marble ceiling supported by sixteenth century lace columns made of a stone that's carved like lace *and is called* lace. *Between the columns were little birds flying in and out, in and out… and there was a tiny rivulet running through the hall with gardenias floating in it.*
—Diana Vreeland, *D.V.*

IF THE ALLURING CUT of an exquisite gown can be compared to the interior architecture of a beautiful room, then the fabric of that garment can be likened to the textures that cover the room's surfaces. Polished materials such as marble and glass, for example, cool to the touch and sleek to the eye, establish an atmosphere of formality; old brick and stamped tin, on the other hand, are warmer, more quaint and informal. Mottled stones or cobblestones, like those in ancient castles, evoke the Old World. Wood beams and plank flooring allude to the provincial, and walls finished in rough plaster can create a Mediterranean-like visual topography. Hand-painting walls in any of a variety of techniques—including ragging, glazing, sponging, and marbleizing—can imbue rooms with Pompeian richness, French ornateness, or classical airiness.

In hot climates, tropicality is accentuated by the feel of cooling terrazzo on bare feet or the use of earthy, hemp-like sisal. In colder regions, slate can be elegantly rustic. A marquetry inlay, on the other hand, looks both intricate and luxurious. Other surfaces achieve jewel-like beauty by using gold- and silver-leaf and precious materials such as malachite and lapis luzuli. Passionate in his belief that it was not so much the particular surface that affected the tone of a room as it was the respect with which it was applied, the architect Louis Kahn wrote, "You can have the same conversation with paper or *papier mâché* or…marble or any material….The beauty of what you create comes if you honor the material for what it is." Plaster, for example, can be treated with the soft elegance of flannel or honored for its aging beauty as it has been in the walls, opposite, and in the exquisite pentimento of Pompeii, overleaf.

Plastering, like most other decorative art forms with roots in ancient cultures, began with the Mesopotamians around 4000 B.C. It took several millennia to develop the skills required to color and shape this combination of lime, sand, and water, and it was the Italians who

14

*A sumptuously decorated wall in the Hermitage, Leningrad, **opposite**.*

*Centuries of weathering have given the walls, **right**, an enduring, melancholy beauty.*

*The stone wall of a Florentine villa is showered with a kaleidoscopic pattern of light and shadow, **left**.*

became Europe's masters of the art. With traditions passed on from their Roman forefathers, they learned to apply as many as eight coats over a foundation wall of sun-dried brick or stone. To the final coat they added white marble powder, which, when blended carefully to retard the setting time, allowed them to model and sculpt the damp plaster into low relief. This process was used for hundreds of years, and, by the Renaissance, the Italians were teaching the English fundamental plastering techniques. Through this knowledge, Palladian, Victorian, and Edwardian homes gained their distinguished plaster reliefs in ceilings, walls and stairways. Influenced by the Celtic love of nature, the British combined classical Italian design with Celtic heraldic foliations, lattice-and-strap work, reed intertwinings, and basket weaves, producing motifs of Gothic intricacy. In France, provincial plastering techniques developed as a protest against the rigidly architectural court style, which had little relevance to popular expression.

*Plaster was impregnated with pigment before being applied to the walls of Linda Chase's home, **above**.*

*The walls of houses in ancient Pompeii, such as those **opposite**, were painted by their owners, poor farmers who wanted to create the illusion of landscape and light in their humble homes. The murals were highly admired by the Pompeians' rich Roman cousins, who imitated them by painting scenes on their marble walls.*

The hand-cut Carrara marble floor, **left**, is the result of a collaboration between interior designer Diane Burn and San Francisco architect Ted Eden. The walls are finished in a three-glaze process, using oil-base paints. The subtle Italian panel motif offsets the deeper celadon green, peaches, and sienna tones of the marble.

Delicate, translucent acid-etched glass enhances the femininity of a San Francisco dressing room setting, **opposite**.

Most of the walls in the Los Angeles house, page 17, were covered with old plaster that had dried and cracked over the years. To replicate this look in two newer rooms, a rough textured plaster was applied to the walls, giving them a sun-bleached, irregular appearance—as if they, too, were covered with years of faded paint, like the stone walls of a Florentine villa, shown on the same page, bleached by the sunlight refracted through a leaded glass window.

*So inviting was the rustic charm of this hand-painted kitchen wall that the katydid, **below**, felt welcome enough to*

*perch on the mottled, cream-colored door surround for hours. To achieve an aged appearance, **opposite**, the walls were hand-painted and distressed with wire brushes, steel wool, and extra fine sandpaper, then "dirty-brushed" overall with umber and sanded again.*

ご ご ご

Surfaces and finishes also enhance the drama of a home by softening or magnifying sound. A needlepoint runner quiets the footsteps that would echo in a marble hallway. Wood floors resound with the activity of life taking place in the house.

Tile, which also amplifies sound, is cool, colorful, and has adorned romantic residences since the time of Alexander the Great, whose chroniclers described splendid decorative bas-reliefs found in Babylon and Persepolis. The Romans, copying the Greeks, favored the use of mosaic tiles on their vaulted ceilings and arches. In Spain, tiles were used to ornament palace walls, floors, window surrounds, wainscoting, fountains, and pools. In fact, they were applied so luxuriously that even the Venetians, renowned romantics and aesthetic adventurers, journeyed to southern Spain to study the complex geometric and foliate tile patterns of such palaces as the Alhambra. In North Africa, a dominant influence on Spanish design, homes and mosques were richly embellished with deep-colored (green, blue, yellow, black, white, and red-brown) mosaics. The Portuguese, hundreds of years after the Spanish and Moroccans first designed with tiles, began using them pictorially, creating large scenes and frames with tile. They depicted court and religious settings and botanical studies, all of which were applied to interior and courtyard walls and benches. The northern Europeans became well known for their folk-patterned tiles that illustrated simple, domestic life.

Toward the end of the nineteenth century, artists, inspired by the fine craftsmanship and elaborate compositions found in tiles made in the East, began to look to the medium as a means of adding exoticism to contemporary design. After centuries of neglect, the arts of tile making, glazing and setting were revived in France, Italy, Spain, Mexico and China.

Evoking the cool serenity of an Italian villa, a marble tile floor, page 18, brings a sense of grandeur to a San Francisco home. This formal elegance complements the ornateness of both the wall mirror and hand-carved seventeenth-century Venetian marble bench. The marble's terra cotta color, reminiscent of the Italian palette, adds warmth to the essentially monochromatic room.

The etched glass used in the dressing room, page 19, prompts images of Paris in the late 1800s. The translucent etched glass panels in the screen, door, and arched window suggest the Belle Epoque. This fanciful touch is echoed by the tracery on the parchment walls and by the lightness of the bleached wood floors.

*The plaster of the wall behind the hand-painted chair, **below**, was painted with a trompe l'oeil wood finish as well as a delicate leaf design. On the "wood"*

Even before the time of Alexander the Great, court craftsmen were using decorative paints, gilding, silver foil, stenciling, and painted friezes and borders to glorify their rulers' great halls of power. Much of their expertise had been passed along from the ancient Egyptian tomb painters and stuccoists, as well as from Persian and Assyrian decorative artists. As cultures grew and declined, vogues in the various arts changed correspondingly. For example, stenciling took

section, several colors were layered across the surface randomly and allowed to dry. Next, a thin coat of grey was applied and then combed with a special brush to produce the look of wood graining. Some areas were rubbed out for a more distressed and irregular pattern.

21

dominance over mural painting during the Middle Ages, and geometric patterns, foils, heraldic motifs, arches, and other architectural references gained in popularity.

In Italy, church and palace commissions kept fresco painters and stencilists at work on designs that often reflected the flamboyance of Byzantine architecture and taste. During the 1500s, richly colored ceilings, bordered by crown moldings, replaced the hanging tapestries, leathers, and silks of the Middle Ages. Eventually, as in so many of the decorative fields, the techniques and styles of Italian artisans gained prominence over the French (a result, in part, of the fact that three French kings—Francis II, Charles IX and Henry III— were sons of Catherine de'Medici). Even the court architecture and ornament of France ultimately absorbed the Italian manner and scale.

To give a Los Angeles kitchen a provincial look, artist Charles Berendt hand-painted the walls, pages 20 and 21, then sanded and scraped them with wire brushes to coarsen the texture. Greyed colors create the impression of wear, tear, and time. The blue-greys and creamy whites also combine well with the warm terra-cotta color of the floor tiles.

Trompe l'oeil (meaning trick of the eye) is a technique by which a flat surface is given the illusion of textural or three-dimensional decoration. It was developed in sixteenth-century Italy, where the Venetians became well known for its use. In France, the artist Fragonard was renowned for his use of this technique in which layers of pigment wash are applied over a ground, usually of creamy grey, followed by the detailed painting of the desired illusion. On page 21, a *trompe l'oeil* wood finish applied to a plaster wall makes a romantic backdrop for an eighteenth-century provincial Italian chair. The rustic quality of the finish contrasts dramatically with the more formal painting on the chair itself and the precise hand-painted branch-and-leaf motif adjoining.

The surface of the armoire, right, was gessoed to give it the appearance of limed oak, a pale look that complements the primitive finish of the ceiling beams. A medallion

*The hand-painted design on the ceiling, **right**, was executed by artist Karin Linder. Its delicate formality provides a graceful transition between the ornate chandelier and the more rustic armoire.*

22

Karin Linder used ground pigments and metallic powders to hand-paint the walls of the bathroom, **left**. She applied an oil-base, high-gloss enamel exterior paint, chosen for its consistency and vibrancy, to create the geometric patterns in the bath, **opposite**. To simulate an aged but once-intense mural, she first scraped the walls with razors, then added detail painting and gold and copper leafing. She finished the process with an oil-base sealer.

design, reminiscent of old Aubusson panels with their cartouche shapes, garlands, and streamers, was hand-painted on the ceiling.

The architecturally appointed master bath in a Manhattan apartment, page 24, called for a stronger look—a geometric design in Pompeian-inspired shapes and colors—copper, juniper, and ginger. The small powder room of the same New York apartment, a room without light or windows, required even stronger colors, preceding page. The domed ceiling and rectangular panels extend the geometric influence while the gargoyle images combine a sense of history with a sense of humor. The faces in the wall design repeat a detail found on the eighteenth-century Italian mirror.

A hand-painted mural creates an air of festivity in the salon of the Spanish villa, opposite. Made to feel like a holiday tent, complete with tassels, the room is enlivened by the mural's color and character.

The glittering interior of a Spanish corridor, right, combines intricately carved and richly colored surfaces. An austere stone floor is balanced by an elaborately carved and gold-leafed ceiling and moldings; the furnishings recede before the flamboyance of the gold and damask-embellished walls. Austerity and extravagance are both characteristic seventeenth-century sensibilities and their resolution in this interior underscores the room's discreet elegance.

The embellishment of surfaces was taken to ornate heights during the eighteenth and nineteenth centuries in the imperial palaces of Russia. The two doors and the wall and column in the Hermitage, shown on the following pages, illustrate the Russian love for color and sumptuous embellishment.

&ebdb; &ebdb; &ebdb;

During the seventeenth century, the French acquired the secrets of Indian fabric printing. The fashion for hanging decorative fabrics on walls led to the development of hand-printed papers, known as *papier peint*—and, ultimately, to what we know now as wallpaper. In England, both Queen Mary and Queen Anne created their own hand-painted floral motifs on wood panels using styles inspired by nature. During the nineteenth century, covering the wall from the baseboard

*A scenic hand-painted wall depicts a fictional landscape in the Spanish salon, **opposite**. The design adds perspective, color and warmth to the room, creating a lighthearted stage for festivity that is enhanced by the* trompe l'oeil *tent motif on the ceiling.*

*The Spanish corridor, **above**, is a tapestry of materials, colors and patterns in which richly colored damask-covered walls combine with intricately carved moldings and an equally elaborate gold-leafed ceiling to give this room its ornate elegance.*

In the Hermitage are a Louis XIV-style
gilt carved and painted door, **above**,
and a French Régence boulle (brass
inlaid with tortoiseshell) door, **opposite**.

28

*A fluted marble column is set into a doré bronze collar atop a bronze ap-plique post, **right**. The wall behind it is made of Norwegian rose marble.*

to the cornice with patterned papers and decorative paper borders became popular. The Victorians were fond of combining handmade wallpapers of various patterns to cover every inch of wall. Architectural papers, called "fresco-papers," simulated panels, cornices, friezes, moldings, and columns in rooms where no architectural elements existed. This fashion was revived in a Philadelphia home, left, where a Fonthill wallpaper combines stripes with a festooned cornice design. In interiors such as the lavish rooms of Russia's Pavlovsk palace, right, where expense posed no restriction, walls were often covered with printed silks.

*The formal staircase, **left**, displays a grand mix of surfaces and finishes that includes a Victorian-style wallpaper and stairs painted with faux finishes.*

*Silk chinoiserie wallpaper covers the walls of a room in Pavlovsk, **opposite**, one of the imperial Russian country palaces.*

Stone and brick, especially when weathered or time worn, add a sense of history to a room. Imbued with curiosity and surprise, the two English drawing rooms, right and overleaf, evoke the romance of ruins. At once humble and expressive, their magic derives from the unexpected: in the room at right, the peeling walls are painted in vivid primary colors; richly ornamental moldings are coupled with a weathered floor; and crumbling surfaces serve as backdrops for distinguished-looking portraits and busts. The next room is a collage of textures and patterns. Ornate moldings are counterpoised against deteriorating brick, plaster, wood, fabric, and paint. Fine antiques and important artworks balance the effect in which accessories are precisely arranged against a backdrop of crumbling chaos.

The mystical mood of the altar room in an Irish castle, page 37, is enhanced by its abundance of primitive surfaces. The rough-hewn ceiling beams, which look as if they could have been felled on the site, make the room feel as if it is located deep in the woods. The randomly composed masonry adds to the air of naturalness, while the six-foot-thick stone walls and carved ornaments heighten the aura of ancestral strength. ಶಿ

*The atmosphere of classicism amidst decay pervades the two English drawing rooms, **right** and **overleaf**. At right, serious artifacts are surrounded by surfaces painted in vivid, crayon-like colors.*

A crumbling fireplace and eroding walls, **above**, amplify the sense of history alluded to by the busts and portraits.

The altar room in the Irish castle, **right**, is a stage for the ritual worship of the goddess Isis. An almost Druidic air is created by the primitive surfaces—stone walls, brick floors and columns, and a crude beam ceiling.

The naked niche—an inviting but odd architectural punctuation, concise and contained, gaping for attention. Should it be filled with *putti*, used to frame a bust? Fitting choices, perhaps, but predictable. Rather, the poetry of this romantic little stage is brought to life when composed with the unexpected.

Like a window display, the niche encourages drama and variety. It is the ideal place to showcase whimsical flower arrangements that can be changed on impulse. The niche shown on these pages is used as a gesture of welcome, an architectural announcement that greets guests with an always fresh and unusual bouquet. Because it holds flowers exclusively, it was bordered with a leaf design, rather than a ribbon or garland or other type of decorative motif.

Above, *a cherub-shaped, terra cotta pot—an inexpensive reproduction of a classical form—was given antique charm by the application of chalk-toned paint inflected with hints of ocher and rouge. The original terra-cotta color on a container this size would have overpowered the muted poetry of the space. The pot has been filled with light pink lysianthus and wonderland white alyssum.*

A NICHE

A three-part terra cotta pot, **top**, holds an assortment of hand-dried flowers and greenery, each bundle tied together with a ribbon of hemp. Soft purple, salmon pink, and sage-green stalks were chosen for the pleasing gradation of color that works harmoniously with the terra-cotta base.

Lending a humorous and literal twist to the classical topiary form, **above**, three moss topiaries—two traditional in shape, one with an unexpected twist— are set in hand-painted pots finished with a crackled glaze and gold-leafed bands.

The quietly animated composition, **top**, mixes the classical with the unexpected. An antique replica of an Etruscan dish is filled with a lawn of moss that provides the arrangement with color and proportion. Startlingly spare, the single stalk with its flowering purple blossom adds a note of surreal poetry.

Two dried rose topiaries make for a duet of contrasts, **above**. The composition juxtaposes a small terra cotta pot in its unpainted state—earthy and modest—with one dressed up in an elegant coat of glaze and two gold bands.

FURNITURE

In keeping with the wish expressed by Her Majesty the Empress, the eight armchairs, six chairs, two screens and the large tables have been covered in poppy-red French silk and decorated with a twist of Italian silk in raspberry red and gold.
> —August Ricard de Montferrand,
> architect to Czar Nicholas I of Russia
> and the Empress Alexandra Feodorovna

COMPOSED OF ARMS, legs, backs, and seats, furniture imitates human shape. From noble and well-appointed to bohemian and casually dressed, individual examples also possess distinct personality. A French *bergère,* for example, has the demeanor of a grand lady; a wing chair appears gentlemanly, while a slipper chair, diminutive and graceful, resembles a ballerina. Planning a room, therefore, can be in many ways like planning a romantic gathering—combining an attractive group of individuals who will keep company not just compatibly, but pleasurably, even excitingly. Will the wallflower respond to the *bon vivant*? Will the *secrétaire abattant* overpower the *récamier*; will the grand piano overpower the ballroom chairs?

In planning the arrangement of furniture in a room, it is advisable to place the strongest pieces first, situating them (either individually or in groups) in a manner that will balance the architecture and establish visual focus. A dominating presence, such as a Biedermeier secretary or a large country *armoire* will dictate the tone of an interior. Less commanding pieces will allow for wider interpretation as well as space for the addition of more furniture. Also, furniture provides a means of introducing interesting finishes and fabrics to a room, touches which accentuate the character of the interior and heighten its romantic appeal.

Left,
from left to right, a painted and caned Louis XVI-style chair, a Venetian-style gilt carved and ebonized framed mirror, and the scrolled arm of an English Regency settee.

Page 41
from left to right, in a room designed by the New York interior designer John Buscarello, are an upholstered grained rosewood récamier settee in the French Empire style; a gilded upholstered open armchair in the Hepplewhite manner with shield back, late eighteenth century; and a carved rosewood pedestal lamp table in the Regency manner.

Left,
at center, a mid-Victorian walnut center table in the Italian Renaissance manner (used for many purposes rather than only as a dining table); a pair of turn-of-the-century gilded carved ballroom side chairs after the Louis XVI style, which are meant to be moved from place to place and are therefore light in weight; encircling the room are mid-Victorian upholstered walnut high-back armchairs in the Gothic style.

Opposite,
at center, an English mahogany antique chest-on-chest with desk drawer in the Chippendale manner, circa 1780; in front, a Chippendale-style corner armchair in ebonized mahogany, circa 1770; to the right, an antique upholstered wingback armchair in the Hepplewhite manner, circa 1780–90.

The sculptural strength of a French Empire *récamier* balances the dramatic draping of the windows and expanse of hand-painted walls in an artist's attic, page 41. Smaller, but equally graceful, furnishings, such as the pedestal table and shield-back armchair, reiterate the *récamier's* elegance.

So stately is almost every piece of furniture in a shrine-like living room in Barcelona, page 42, that the setting bears an aura of papal grandeur. The Gothic Victorian armchair and side chairs are upholstered in a Renaissance-gold velvet which, like the ornate woodwork on the center table, adds to the room's majesty.

A tattered grandeur is the hallmark of the library in an Irish castle, page 43. The late-eighteenth-century English chest-on-chest stores generations of family records. The serious, well-used mien of the piece suits the room, as does the nicked and scuffed late-eighteenth-century mahogany corner chair in front of it.

A gentleman's library chair, draped with a silk scarf, and a circular game table modestly furnish one corner of an English drawing room, left. The cribbage board, globe, and candlelight add to the quiet gentility of the room.

Left,
in the foreground, an English country-style gentleman's library armchair; at rear, a game table with set-in cribbage board in the English country manner.

Opposite,
from left to right, in a room designed by Ronald Bricke: an Italian Renaissance-style carved, gilded bishop's stool with "X" frame, late nineteenth century; a pair of upholstered mahogany armchairs in the French Empire manner with gilded, carved dragons; a William IV marquetry-inlay ebonized center table with intarsia (ivory) inlay edge from the latter half of the nineteenth century; at center, an Oriental-style carved, ebonized, and gilded tea table with overall incised carvings, late nineteenth century.

Large-scale French Empire, Italian Renaissance and English furniture give the formally composed living room, **previous page**, a look of masculine elegance. The imposing weight of the pieces is softened by the colorful fabrics with which they are upholstered and by the gracefully scrolled curves of the chair backs.

Although the desire to make a home comfortable would seem to have been prevalent throughout Western history, after the days of antiquity, it did not actually re-emerge until the seventeenth century. In *Ivanhoe*, Sir Walter Scott described the interior of a medieval castle by intoning, "Magnificence there was, with some rude attempt at taste; but of comfort there was little, and, being unknown, it was unmissed." An appetite for ease arose with the manifestation of the world of the family and the appreciation of the house as a setting for an emerging life of internal reflection. The writer John Lakacs explains that "as the self-consciousness of medieval people was spare, the interiors of their houses were bare, including the halls of nobles and of kings. The interior furniture of houses appeared together with the interior furniture of minds."

It was not until the eighteenth century that a marriage of comfort and luxury occurred in the design of interiors—and in furniture. Particularly in France, voluptuous curves and lush upholstery replaced the rigid angularity of earlier furnishings, and sumptuousness became the fashion. Less massive and more shapely, less formal and more animated, furniture, for the first time, grew feminine in spirit, an influence, partially, of the women of the salons. The living room in the San Francisco home of fashion designer Jessica McClintock, right, exemplifies this approach with its abundance of plush, graceful furnishings arranged within a pristinely monochromatic setting.

*In the formal living room designed by Diane Burn, **right**, are a pair of Louis XVI-style bergères in front of the fireplace opposite which are a pair of Louis XV-style bergères. A pair of Victorian club-style sofas flank the marble-topped tables made from Corinthian capitals.*

*In a room, **left**, designed by Robert Metzger, Inc. of New York is an uphol-stered mahogany récamier in the French Empire manner, late nineteenth century; at left, an oval mahogany sewing table in the French Empire manner, raised on gilded dragon legs, early nineteenth century.*

A boudoir by the New York interior designer Noel Jeffery, **right**, is furnished with a Louis XV-style upholstered marquis *chair* and a Victorian club-style sofa.

The meticulously appointed Empire-style room on page 48 brings to mind the French classicism of Napoleon Bonaparte, who was intent on creating an image of Roman imperial majesty for his régime. Napoleon sought a style totally distinct from the more feminine and luxurious furniture designs of those that preceded his reign. It is not hard to imagine an emperor in repose in this massive, late-nineteenth-century *récamier*, set beneath a gilt-framed military painting.

Equally aristocratic, but obviously feminine, is the sitting room of a New York boudoir, page 49, where sleek, elegantly upholstered furnishings, all in white, provide a glamorous backdrop for a treasured portrait.

& otilde;   õ   õ

In the living room of her New York City *pied-à-terre*, left, Linda Chase placed a late-nineteenth-century daybed prominently as a poetic setting for reading books, napping, and antique-doll tea parties. The decorative carving and gold-leaf detailing on the daybed balance its architectural severity, while its irregular painted finish harmonizes with the variety of objects surrounding the piece. The oval-backed antique Louis XVI-style chairs and the lozenge-shaped banquette serve as rounded counterpoints to the squares and rectangles of the mirror, screen, daybed, and pillows.

In an artist's attic, next page, the fluid lines and compatible proportions of the Portuguese rosewood commode, Italian armchair, and Victorian pedestal harmonize their composition. The gilded detailing shared by the pieces also unifies the arrangement.

*In Linda Chase's New York living room, **left**, are a French Empire-style painted and carved daybed, a Louis XVI-style banquette with Aubusson upholstery, and a pair of Louis XVI-style upholstered chairs.*

Left,
from left to right, in a room designed by New York interior designer John Buscarello: a Victorian bust of the god Mercury on a Victorian pedestal; a Portuguese rosewood commode, mid-eighteenth century; a gilded, upholstered armchair in the Hepplewhite manner with shield back, late eighteenth century.

Opposite,
at center, a Vargueño cabinet on a stand in the Italian Renaissance manner with a tortoise and fruitwood facade with bronze appliques, on top of which stands a Victorian patinated bronze figural clock, early nineteenth century. The Vargueño is derived from the medieval hutch or treasure chest. The fruitwood library table is in the Italian country manner, late eighteenth century.

After the turmoil of the Dark Ages, monasteries provided a setting for a tranquil and settled way of life, a serenity that is translated to a study in Barcelona, shown on the previous page. Sparsely furnished and decorated with personal and religious artifacts, the room is pervaded by a monastic serenity. The Vargueño cabinet at center has an altar-like presence that is enhanced by the carved wood sculpture of the Madonna and Child atop it, as well as by its elaborate detailing. Even the table lamp, which is evocative in shape, color, and ornamentation of an ecclesiastical cap, alludes to worship.

An ethereal aura also illuminates the setting, left, in which a lyre-back side chair rests beneath an Old Master painting of an angel. The chair's lyrical shape is a visual intimation of celestial harmony, just as the curvilinear helmet of the wrought-iron *torchère* to the left evokes images of medieval knights.

The large French country *armoire*, opposite, was the perfect size and proportion to fill the space between the two doorway openings of a living room. Its curved bonnet and molded scrolls soften the angularity of the French doors, while its fruitwood veneer harmonizes with the wood floor.

ॐ   ॐ   ॐ

Iron, which was rare in the ancient civilizations of the Eastern Mediterranean, was considered as precious as the gold, silver, stones, and enamel then used in making decorative objects and small implements. It took nearly a millennium (until the Romanesque era—between the eleventh and thirteenth centuries) before it became pervasive in the making of romantic ornaments such as rosettes, heraldic crests and animals, crosses, scrolls, *quatrefoils*, *fleurs-de-lis*, and *palmettes*. Today, wrought iron is favored by designers of

*In a setting composed by Linda Chase, **above**, is a painted and carved lyre-back side chair in the Louis XVI manner, latter half, nineteenth century; a patinated wrought-iron torchère floor lamp in the Italian Renaissance manner with lantern helmet shade, mid-nineteenth century.*

***Opposite**, from left to right, are an upholstered bergère in the Louis XV manner, early nineteenth century; an upholstered-seat banquette in the Regency manner with gilded rope-turned frame, late nineteenth century; a fruitwood armoire in the French-country Louis XV manner, with molded scroll-panel doors, latter half, eighteenth century; painted and upholstered daybed in the Louis XV manner, late nineteenth century.*

romantic furniture not only because of these historical associations, but also because of the ease with which it accommodates itself to curves and because of the beauty of its patinas, which are enhanced by time and weather.

The chipped-paint finish on the French wrought-iron banquette, below, has been left to contrast with the piece's rich upholstery and formal trim. This play between crude and refined surfaces is mirrored in the rough clay-tile floor, which has been embellished with gold-leaf grout. Opposite, the lacy scrollwork on a late-nineteenth-century wrought-iron pastry table offsets the linearity of the same tiles, while its honed marble top harmonizes with the color of the floor. The blue-green patina of wrought iron adds a French/Italian tone to the palette.

The singular placement of a nineteenth-century *fauteuil*, page 58, accentuates its individuality in a formal interior. Its bleached finish harmonizes with the pale palette of the setting.

A contemporary twist on classicism, the bronze *chaise longue*, page 59, was inspired by Botticelli's *Birth of Venus*. Its patina, "encouraged" by allowing the bronze to oxidize in sunlight, contributes to the piece's timeless character.

ॐ   ॐ   ॐ

On page 60, a Victorian gentleman's wardrobe interrupts an ocean of blue painted on the walls of a Long Island summer cottage. The room's offbeat air comes from the placement of so imposing a piece of furniture in so relaxed a setting. Similarly unexpected is the solitary grace of the English Queen Anne chair, on the same page, set against rustic, sun-bleached shutters in a Spanish salon.

The dining room in an English farmhouse, page 61, presents a picture of generations of gentle domesticity with its abundance of much-used, much-loved late-eighteenth-century furniture. The simple, solid furnishings, from the bow-shaped pine and sycamore settle and small, curved tavern table to the country-style open hutch—all look as if they had been built to last forever.   ॐ

*A French-style painted wrought-iron banquette, **left**, with double-scroll legs, mid-nineteenth century.*

*A French painted wrought-iron "pastry" table, **opposite**, with a marble top and fleur-de-lis crenulated apron and scroll legs, late nineteenth century; a dressing stool in the Louis XVI manner with a painted, carved frame, late nineteenth–early twentieth century.*

A Venetian-style carved and painted fauteuil, *circa 1860,* **left**.

A bronze chaise longue by New Orleans designer Mario Villa, **right**. The pillows reiterate the chaise's shell form and soften the spare setting.

An English Queen Anne-style side chair with fiddle back, late nineteenth century, **left**.

An early-Victorian gentleman's dressing cabinet, **below**, with a flat molded cornice and arched, paneled doors, mid-nineteenth century.

A bow-shaped Colonial-style pine and sycamore settle, late eighteenth century; a curved tavern tea table, late eighteenth century; a late-eighteenth-century country-style sideboard with majolica and English pearlware and sycamore and fruitwood scoops, **right**.

EMBELLISHING WITH TASSELS

*The large late-eighteenth-century Italian armoire, **top**, called for an embellishment as elaborate as the ornate carving on the piece itself. The tassel, made of antique bronze metallic threads, was chosen for both its intricacy and shape: its appliquéd crown mirrors the curvilinear shape at the top of the armoire; the beaded detail at the bottom repeats the detailing along the door.*

*The hand-painted cupboard, **above**, was embellished with silk tassels bound with antique gold cord as a means of softening the cupboard's strong linear character. The bright rose-colored tassels enliven the piece's palette and introduce a note of humor by being hung in an unexpected place—on the hinges.*

Just as beautiful buttons "finish" a jacket and ribbons adorn the hair, tassels add a flourish that "dresses" a piece of furniture. Although they demand no extraordinary thought or expertise, they are signs of extravagance—detailing that implies lavish taste and exhibits extra care.

Rather than a tailored button or a flowery rosette, pairs of tassels were added to the pillows on the graceful French daybed, **above**. Unusually intense colors were selected to emphasize the detailing and to add contrast.

ACCESSORIES

For a time the most famous room in Russia was the Empress's mauve boudoir. Everything in it was mauve: curtains, carpet, pillows, even the furniture was mauve-and-white Hepplewhite. Masses of fresh white and purple lilacs, vases of roses and orchids and bowls of violets perfumed the air. Tables and shelves were cluttered with books, papers, porcelains and enamels....In this cozy room, surrounded by her treasured objects, Alexandra felt secure.

—Robert K. Massie
Nicholas and Alexandra

ACCESSORIES INTRODUCE IDEAS, shapes, color, pattern, and romantic personality to a room. They reveal the interests and character of those who inhabit a home and add narrative richness to its ambience. Travel mementos and maps, for example, suggest adventure in faraway lands; heirlooms impart a sense of history; and keepsakes such as a dancer's shoes or old hats illustrate personal tastes and passions. Some accessories, such as dolls or a glass menagerie,

A rare late-nineteenth-century icon of "the Veronica Veil" from northern Mexico hangs above a tableau of Latin American icons collected by the New Orleans designer Mario Villa. At center is an 1878 Mexican painting of St. Augustine, a mystical force in the Catholic church.

lighten the tone of a room. Needlepoint pillows and footstools add comfort. Flowers, plants, and topiaries breathe beauty into a home while screens provide mystery by creating the illusion (or reality) of something hidden.

Carved and painted icons, cherished for their mystical magnetism, are arranged in a composition, at left that mixes primitive images from northern Mexico with those that are more baroque, from Central America.

The beauty of foliate patterns, both carved and painted, provides a lyrical undertone for an arrangement of accessories in the apartment, opposite. A scrollwork of vines embellishes the eighteenth-century hand-painted Venetian table. The motif is repeated in the carved leaf designs on the nineteenth-century tureen and carved wooden lamp base. (They appear also in the carved relief of the *trumeau* behind.) In harmony with these pieces is a playful display of four classic Italian seventeenth-century *putti*, representing the four seasons.

64

Pillows evoke sensuality and create comfort. The harems of the Near East were strewn with exquisitely embroidered silk pillows, and in Spain, even after Renaissance styles were adopted, women preferred to sit on cushions on the floor, after the Moorish fashion, rather than on chairs. Soft and plush, pillows ultimately represented privilege. Well beyond medieval times, when none but royalty could be seated in the rulers' company, monarchs and nobles were given the added luxury of a pillow against which to recline.

The Aubusson pillows on the window seat, left, soften the altar-like arrangement of accessories above it: surrounded by two wrought-iron candlesticks is an eighteenth-century hand-carved *putto*, originally part of an Italian altar. The colors of the cherub—bronze and terra cotta—are repeated in the pillows. Trimming the Aubusson is a nineteenth-century gold fabric that adds elegance to the composition. A pleated paneling dresses the pillows, below, also made of

Seventeenth-century carved wood putti, ***previous page****, representing the four seasons, a nineteenth-century Wedgwood Queensware tureen, and a lamp whose base is made from a nineteenth-century carved-wood altar stick, are arranged on an eighteenth-century lacquered table made in Venice. In keeping with the festival atmosphere of that city, the rococo furniture produced there was distinctly theatrical, and here, provides a colorful setting for the monochromatic accessories arranged on it.*

Aubusson pillows, ***above left and right****, add to the richness and delicacy of a setting in Linda Chase's Los Angeles home. The curvilinear design of the candlesticks mirrors the scrolls in the Aubusson pattern just as the candlestick chains repeat the garlands in one pillow. The pleated border on the pillows has been left deliberately without trim because of the intricacy of the Aubusson design itself.*

The fireplace, **above**, is obviously well loved and well used. Although it contains two classic late-eighteenth-century brass andirons designed with scrolled feet and steeple finials on turned posts, there is no screen to hide fire, logs, or ashes. This wantonness is offset by the formal arrangement to the right of an early-nineteenth-century cartouche-shaped antique Venetian mirror and Waterford girondole, before which stands a Louis XVI-style chair. Both the weathered fairground horse and worn tapestry, spread across the floor, lighten the overall mood of the room.

A Napoleonic doré bronze columned mantel clock, circa 1800, **opposite,** with Imperial eagle from Petrodvorets, Peter the Great's summer palace. The urn beside it is Vieux Paris porcelain made around 1800.

A Louis XVI gilt and patinated bronze mantel clock with an enameled face from Pavlovsk, **above,** one of the Russian Imperial family's country palaces. It is embellished with figures of maidens and a putto and dates from around 1800.

A French Empire doré bronze mantel
clock with allegorical figures, **opposite**,
set atop a black marble base with an
inset gilt bronze plaque of classical relief
figures, from Petrodvorets, circa 1800.

A French Empire doré bronze mantel
clock with allegorical figures gazing at
bust of a classical sage, circa 1800,
above, from the Hermitage.

71

elaborate Aubusson. The pleating reiterates the formality of the fabric, while the simple round shape, devoid of cording, makes an eloquent frame for the antique tapestry.

Aubusson weaving comes from the French town of the same name which has been an acclaimed tapestry-making center since the fourteenth century. During the mid-1700s, just when the desire for comfort arrived in high society, the sources for Turkish and Persian carpets diminished, and Aubusson's manufacturers began producing woven rugs. Known for the exquisite complexity of their patterns and their meticulous workmanship, Aubusson tapestries and carpets were commissioned by the French monarchs (Napoleon spent three million francs at Aubusson in the year 1806 alone) and eventually became, like many other examples of decorative art, potent status symbols among the gentry.

Completely unlike a fine Aubusson, yet as romantically subtle, is the woven carpet in the English drawing room on page 67, which, though nearly threadbare, lightens the mood of the dark-walled room and reads like a tapestry spread across the floor. This look of tattered elegance is continued by the other accessories, from the weathered fairground horse to the basket of wild twigs in front of the fireplace, which, like most hearths, is the focus of the room. Despite the formality of the traditional landscape painting above it and the elegant tableau with crystal candlesticks to its right, the fireplace casts a glow of warm disarray.

   ॐ   ॐ   ॐ

Marking the moment, clocks are reminders of the ephemeral nature of romance (and there is perhaps no more indulgent token of luxury than an expensive clock that doesn't keep time). Whether mounted within sculptural frameworks, gilded, enameled, or decorated with jewels and

A mid-eighteenth-century portrait of a noblewoman in the manner of Gainsborough gives stately grace to a spare English room, **left.** *Inside the hearth stands a pair of mid-eighteenth-century brass andirons with double scroll legs and beehive finials on turned posts.*

73

other ornaments, clocks are commanding *objets d'art* and were seriously collected by the European and Russian monarchs. Floor, mantel, and table clocks from the eighteenth and nineteenth centuries, manufactured in the workshops of France, England, and Germany, decorate the grand palaces of Russia. The examples on pages 68 through 71 illustrate the tastes of the Russian monarchs for French clocks (which were considered the finest) in the forms of classical temples and allegorical scenes. Others were fashioned to resemble vases, lyres, and chariots, or were sculpted in bas relief with images of muses, gods, goddesses, heroes and heroines. Some bear musical mechanisms that play airs by Mozart and Haydn. Since the Renaissance, when clocks came into vogue as decorative accessories, artists have been challenged to transcend the regimentation of minute-marking timepieces. Some created examples embellished with sculptural dancers who performed on the hour, others devised clocks that chimed at the change of seasons. Of all clocks, however, the most romantic is the sundial, which can be read only at the whim of the clouds.

      Rooms need not be decorated abundantly to be romantic. Sometimes a few simple accessories make them all the more dramatic, as in the English drawing room on the previous page where the portrait over the fireplace derives its strength from its singularity. The logs below, though seeming to be carelessly stacked, are symmetrically composed. Also formally balanced are the small bouquet at the letter-writing desk at left and the large spray of flowers that brightens the dim corner at right. In the English foyer, right, the starkness of the wall and the strength of the architectural detailing—door frame and bannister—are offset by the whimsical character of a rocking horse and the strong medieval persona of the carved floor clock.

*The English foyer, **right**, is decorated simply with an English carved oak tall-case clock with knights in armor carved in the Elizabethan manner, and a turn-of-the-century folk-art painted and decorated wood rocking horse. The rocking horse, which suggests movement, enhances the repetitive rhythm of the design of the Elizabethan-style wrought-iron bannister and its elaborate newel posts.*

74

A mix of English, Dutch, and Spanish accessories accounts for the casual charm of the English farmhouse, left, owned by a couple with a passion for collecting folk antiques. An eighteenth-century Act-of-Parliament clock dominates a corner of their "Inglenook" room, while in the dining room, below left, wood finishes, both painted and natural, provide a warm backdrop for a diverse collection of folkish accessories. Collected objects relating to the home and childhood reinforce the warm domesticity of the living room, opposite.

Antique books and a professorial antique doll transform a previously undefined corner of a room into a library-like fantasy, overleaf. Since the doll sits on the shelf, rather than on a chair or elsewhere, he looks like a dapper Einstein pausing to read his miniature book by sunlight. The abandoned lorgnette in the foreground prompts wonder as to who might have been studying at this desk.

In Linda Chase's New York *pied à terre*, page 79, an assortment of more refined but equally whimsical accessories has found order. Dolls are posed on steps; books, boxes, and decanters are arranged on a desk; mirrors and paintings frame a curtained doorway; and, in the background, pink peonies contribute to a concert of color in a dressing room draped in floral and striped fabrics.

*To the right of the eighteenth-century Act-of-Parliament clock in an English farmhouse, **above**, is a seventeenth-century Spanish carved wooden figure, and to its left a tole corner cabinet. The architectural quality of the early-eighteenth-century English-country painted tall-case clock, **opposite**, offsets the folk appeal of the late-eighteenth-century painted rooster weathervane, baskets, toys, pair of mid-eighteenth-century hammered-brass candle sconces and other homey accessories. **Left**, a turn-of-the-century rocking horse adds child-like fantasy to a domestic scene established by the display of an eclectic collection of Delft, Canton and other ceramic plates and pitchers on an early-eighteenth-century English hutch buffet. A still life of fruit in an early-eighteenth-century English-country wood mixing bowl enhances the folk atmosphere.*

A French Empire-style bronze boulliotte *lamp* with tole shade decorates a library desk, **left**. *The coffee cup and saucer are Vieux Paris, 1800-1820.*

A symmetrical arrangement of mirrors and paintings in antique, gilded, carved wood frames surrounds the draped passageway, **opposite**. An eighteenth-century Mme. de Pompadour doll in a shadowbox keeps company with the antique dolls grouped on the steps below.

French bronze jewel boxes with inset miniature paintings on ivory, a mid-seventeenth-century classic Italian gessoed wood putto, a silver perfume decanter and antique books embossed in gold suggest luxury and femininity in the grouping of accessories, **opposite**.

The white antique lace curtain provides a delicate contrast to the rough plaster wall surface, **right,** against which are set a French eighteenth-century planter and a medieval-looking candle sconce with rusted finish.

*The ornateness of the antique French mirrors, **opposite** and **right,** is dramatized by the rough plaster wall.*

One of the *putti* shown in a grouping of accessories on page 63 has been used in a very different, yet equally lyrical arrangement on page 80. Combined with a vase of roses in full bloom and a collection of French bronze jewel boxes and silver perfume decanters, the scene expresses an elegant femininity. The books stacked behind the cherub, who is caught in a gesture of offering, prompts thoughts of sonnets. The bouquet, sent perhaps by a suitor, is mirrored in the delicate floral motif of the Aubusson tablecovering and in the hand-painted decoration of the gold-mesh-trimmed vase.

A bouquet of flowers, held in an eighteenth-century French planter, rather than in a vase, page 81, suggests a garden brought inside. Mirroring the glory of the potted snapdragons are the flowers peeking in from a window box.

The contrast of a precisely clipped topiary and a freely growing rose bush, page 82, illustrates yet another approach to decorating a table or corner with flowers. The topiary repeats the round shape of the poufs in the valance above it, while the roses reflect the color of the table square. The nineteenth-century antique trims and tassels on the curtain and tablecovering echo the gold finishes on the mirror, miniature, and chair frames to the left.

Mirrors, like romance, indulge our romantic vanity, create illusion, reflect the corners and vistas of our private worlds, and entice us to see ourselves as we hope to be seen. Found in important homes throughout Europe in the seventeenth century, the mirror was a sign of wealth and prestige. As time went on it came to be appreciated for its ability to bring more light into a room—doubling and re-doubling the power of lamps and candles at night and amplifying the sunlight from a window. The mirror freed the upper-class domestic interior from its need to concentrate furniture around the window, and enabled tables and chairs to be arranged more freely throughout a room.

The ornate eighteenth-century hand-carved mirror, preceding pages, creates a double illusion by reflecting an antique mirror opposite it. The cartouche-shaped looking glass at right was chosen for its elaborate detailing, which corresponds to the intricate ornamental carving on its stand. Designed as part of the free-standing screen, the mirror, opposite, turns a sculptural decoration that could be used in almost any room into an ideal dressing-room accessory. ❧

A dressing mirror, **opposite**, dates from the nineteenth century. The mirror, **above**, was incorporated as part of the glazed wood screen designed by Bell' occhio of San Francisco.

A bow of antique gold-wire mesh displays an eighteenth-century porcelain miniature showing Louis XVI as a young dauphin in a 22-karat gold-leafed period hand-carved frame, **left**. Fabric of a darker gold color than that of the frame harmonizes with the deeper hues found in the painting's background, creating a transition between the two tones. A length of ribbon extends from the bottom of the frame to elongate the proportions of the composition and to reiterate the length of the oval shape.

D elicate in detail and diminutive in proportion, miniatures are touched with the romance of childhood. Their small size imparts a sense of the endearing to a home. Easier to arrange on walls and shelves than standard-size art, they also can be moved simply from one room to another. Miniatures are engaging whether displayed alone or massed in picturesque groupings. The examples shown here use ribbons, bows, and antique frames to tie the compositions together elegantly. ঌ❧

MINIATURES

The strong, precise geomtery of the frame, **top left**, offsets the feminine delicacy of a portrait of Mme. de Pompadour. The frame is hung on an unexpectedly wide piece of gold mesh and embellished with an antique gold tassel whose starburst head was intended for use on upholstery.

An antique Italian picture frame, **top right**, anchored to the wall with eighteenth-century gold mesh, displays one eighteenth-century miniature on a bracket while showcasing a second

within its borders. Suspended from the frame is a symmetrical grouping of three eighteenth-century courtesans. Because mixing compositional directions enlivens visual interest, the arrangement has been placed on the wall at a point where the diagonal sweep of the hand-painted wall design is in strongest contrast to vertical and horizontal frames.

An antique hand-painted Italian frame, dressed with an antique gold-mesh bow, **above left**, displays five porcelain

miniatures. The smallest has been hung to appear as a pendant dangling from the bow, even though it is actually mounted. Antique gold cord lines the inside edge of the frame.

Although not identically matched in shape or size, the eighteenth-century French pastel portrait miniatures in the collection at **above right** appear to be symmetrically arranged, an effect that is accentuated by the uniformity of the frame colors. The crown on the top miniature dictated its placement.

CURTAINS AND DRAPERY

Also marvelous in a room is the light that comes through the windows and that belongs to that room....Just think, that we can claim a slice of the sun. —Louis Kahn
Between Silence and Light

CURTAINS CONTRIBUTE to the romantic mystique by softening a room's edges—dressing the windows and draping the doorways. Closing out the world, they enhance intimacy and, historically, have been both symbols of intrigue and signs of privilege. The Caesars, subject to the open interiors of their day, retired behind curtains to ponder the cares of empire in solitude. The medieval gentry, living in the communal chaos of an extended family, used curtains to conduct their personal and business affairs out of sight of the domestic throng. Lace panels and beaded curtains were favored by courtesans and women of the harem who wished to see without being seen.

Since antiquity, curtains have been hung everywhere from houses and tents to carriages and sedan chairs.

*Hand-spun silk has been folded, draped, and looped through eighteenth-century curtain fittings and gathered with antique metallic mesh, **above**.*

The first examples were simple pieces of fabric draped over a horizontal pole attached to a wall. Their design grew more complex as interiors became more decorative. Eventually, the curtain was elaborated upon with swags (loose, graceful vertical drapings of fabric), festoons (curving, garland-like, horizontal drapings), and valances (horizontal decorative borders framing the top).

Light, veil-like curtains were preferred in the hot climates of the East where the flowing of air between shadowy rooms was as important as the caress of silk against skin. In Europe, the heavy damask and velvet curtains of the Renaissance eventually gave way to silks and satins. In late-eighteenth-century France, when the popularity of imported muslins and printed cottons began to jeopardize the country's textile industry, Emperor Napoleon revived production by ordering from the factories of Lyons enormous quantities of Imperial-yellow and emerald-green silk, deep crimson and classical white satin, and brocades adorned with metallic threads.

*An Austrian shade adds formality to a Miami breakfast room designed by Gloria Calhoun, **previous page**.*

*The fullness of the folds of the drapery designed by John Buscarello, **above**, softens the odd angles of the architecture of an attic room. The drapery's curves also mirror the lines of the settee.*

*The window dressing, **right**, designed by San Francisco interior designer Paul Vincent Wiseman combines a patterned chintz (the same used in the upholstery of the sofas) with a sheer chintz. Its overall effect matches the formality of the high-ceilinged salon.*

The curtains and draperies of the French aristocracy were renowned for their intricate beauty and exclusivity. However, because their production techniques, which required great expertise in cutting and application, were kept secret even from apprentices, the court style never reached the populace, and, instead, the common people continued to dress their windows with fabric hung from simple valances.

Swagged and draped curtains were introduced into English drawing rooms in the eighteenth century, and by the nineteenth, curtains and drapery could be found commonly in parlors, dining rooms, and master bedrooms (a holdover from the eighteenth-century custom of entertaining in the best bedchamber). During the Victorian era, windows were often draped with two panels—lace or another sheer fabric hanging straight to the floor with a second fabric swagged or draped over it.

Doorway curtains, *portières,* have, like window curtains, long been used for privacy and insulation. In more recent centuries they were appreciated for their graceful folds and opulent fabrics such as damasks, brocades, and needlepoints. When hung in the doorway of a salon, parlor, library, or dining room, two different fabrics were generally used, each finished and embellished to correspond with the color and style of the room it faced. In nineteenth-century Europe, as foreign trade and the taste for exoticism grew, *portières* were made from Indian shawls, Turkish carpets, and even silk dresses, pieced together into panels.

A sheer Austrian shade, page 89, invites the morning sunlight into the breakfast room of a Florida home. The delicacy of its silk complements the femininity of the lace table covering, and the ruffled repetition of its curves softens the angularity of the window frame.

A gracefully effective drapery, page 90, was designed to conceal the harsh edges of a wall opening. Its swag, a variation on the traditional jabot, is made of an Italian printed cotton, lined with green silk damask. The floor-to-ceiling cascade of fabric dramatizes the entire setting.

In the spacious setting on pages 90 and 91, a delicate window dressing was devised to complement the formality of the room without obscuring the beauty of the windows with heavy drapery. A *trompe l'oeil* motif, inspired by a Neopolitan wall mural, was painted on the wood valances under which patterned and sheer chintzes were draped.

Neoclassical in its simplicity and opulent in its effect is the simply swagged curtain, opposite, that covers the walls of a New York living room. No expense was spared in hanging the dove-grey silk, tent-like, from corner to corner, relaxing the linearity of the room. The bronze fittings that hold the curtain to the wall complement the detailing on the *secrétaire abattant.*

Neoclassical fashions, such as these, as well as the even more lavish baroque, were highly indulged by the aristocracy of Imperial Russia, who spared no expense when it came to the furnishing and decoration of their palaces and manor houses. For example, the luxurious silk brocade *portière* on page 94 adds even greater elegance to a door embellished with gold leaf. Swags of eighteenth-century gold-threaded fringe are anchored to the curtain with bronze mesh bows from which tassels are hung by gold braid. On page 95, an Austrian shade in deep claret silk coupled with a formal shirred panel in the shape of an arc formally showcases an exquisite neoclassical urn. The iridescent cast of the swagged green silk curtains on page 96 set off the muted peach tones of the surrounding wall decorated with *grisaille* painting. Elaborate swags of crimson silk brocade balance in dramatic gesture and brilliant color the baroque intricacy of the gilded carved wood detailing above them, page 97.

The freely poufed curtains in a sitting room, and music room, page 98, are as romantic as eighteenth-century ballgowns. Made from hundreds of yards of taffeta, they are simply but thickly gathered at the top and tied with rolled fabric. In the dressing room, page 99, lace over lace was used for an airier, more delicate effect. The lavishly full table skirt is French cotton lace over taffeta.

The tailored softness of Austrian shades in silk canvas, subdue the architectural linearity of a Manhattan bedroom, page 100. The effect is an engaging combination of simplicity and extravagance. A shirred silk panel elegantly bands the shades across the top.

For centuries, tie-backs have been part of the dressing of windows, niches, doorways, and beds. In fact, their use is considered so refined a decorative touch that in France the creation of *passementerie,* intricately designed tassels of fine silk and metallic threads, is a distinct art form. Tradi-

The walls of a room designed by Robert Metzger Interiors, Inc. have been draped with a subtly patterned fabric and anchored with hardware in a neoclassical motif, **opposite.**

The intricately patterned fabric of the portière, **left**, *extends the ornateness of the gold-leafed door in Pavlovsk.*

94

A shirred fabric panel crowns a valance in Peter the Great's summer palace, **right**.

*Delicate swags of muted green, rose, and cream silk, **left**, accent a niche bordered by walls painted in intricate* trompe l'oeil.

*Yards of crimson silk have been gathered into an elegant pendant shape, **right**, creating curves that soften the ornate geometry of the gold-leafed wall above.*

*The voluminous curtains, **left**, and **above**, heighten the grandeur of the rooms. Designer Diane Burn allowed them to balloon onto the floor to extend the aura of luxury. She used tassels to punctuate the diaphanous expanse of lace curtains, **opposite**.*

The linen Austrian shades, **above**, designed by Linda Chase, add a rhythmic liveliness to a Manhattan bedroom.

Indulging her signature love of romantic color, Linda Chase used the same vibrant pink for both curtains and cushion upholstery, **right** .

tionally, tie-backs have been made of fabric either identical to or contrasting with the curtain, of braided cord and rope, their designs based on geometrics, florets, and fans. However, anything attractive can be used to tie back a curtain, be it a garland of flowers or a carved wooden ornament.

ॐ   ॐ   ॐ

Linda Chase created three romantic curtain variations for her Los Angeles home. On page 102, hand-spun silk is symmetrically draped over lace to evoke the pomp and femininity of medieval costume. The curtain's poufs suggest the sleeves or bust of an Elizabethan dress. The eighteenth-century bronze-mesh ribbon that bands and secures the curtains resembles the ribbons of honorary medals, adding a note of ceremony to the design.

A graceful, pure white, mantilla-like curtain, right and below, evokes the majestic piety of a Spanish woman at prayer. Made from antique lace, it was tacked to the wall with the medallion design centered in the window frame. A lace table square takes the place of a shade.   ॐ

*The white silk-over-lace curtains, **left**, are as ceremonious and enchanting as a wedding gown.*

*The simple draping of an elaborately detailed fabric, **above right**, is dramatized by its placement against a highly textured wall, **right**.*

With the exception, perhaps, of moonlight, no illumination creates a romantic ambience like candlelight. Mysterious and mystical, the gleam of tapers provokes a mood of reflection. Just as its softness encourages ease, its flickering is a reminder of the ephemeral. In candlelight, not everything is revealed at once: like romance itself, the shadows it casts are as alluring as its glow.

Candlesticks and candle-holding wall sconces lend romance to any room both by virtue of their presence and through their singular beauty. Poised like ladies-in-waiting, decorative even when unlit, candles add an expectant air to the decor. Antique examples—embellished with historical motifs or fanciful filigree—further enhance the dramatic aura of a room lit by candlelight.

*The Victorian bronze candelabrum, **left**, was originally part of an altar. Here it is used as the focus of a simple tableau. The curve of its swagged chains is mirrored in the painted drapery of a marionette stage at right.*

WITH CANDLES

An antique tall-clock pendulum has been reshaped to serve as a wall sconce, **top left**. The candle arm was added to hold a single taper. The simplicity of the sconce's design offsets its complex relief pattern, just as the ornament's rusty surface creates an interesting juxtaposition of texture with the slickness of a waxy candle.

The more primitive wrought-iron Portuguese candelabrum, **top right**, is amusing for its attempt at regal allusion. Symmetrical and incorporating an English-style medallion, it gives the impression of importance while retaining a rustic character. Its visual contradictions are a great part of its appeal.

The bronze ormolu swinging-arm sconce candleholder, **above left**, one of a pair, can be moved away from the wall when lit. Candles of different heights were used deliberately: the taller one next to the picture frame works as a transition between the long linear stroke of the frame and the more distant shorter one. A symmetrical composition of candles in an identical sconce on the other side of the painting (not shown) actually frames the frame.

The once-electrified, hand-painted eighteenth-century tole lantern, **above right**, has been returned to its original, pre-electric charm. A candle was added in place of a filament, and, after a mirror on the backplate of the inside was removed, the surface was distressed and silver-leafed to produce a softer glow than the glare generated by the mirror.

B E D S

The royal bed had been built on a platform that reached out over a lake and was made of alternating bricks of ruby, emerald, silver and gold. Over the bed hung a veil of green silk held by four pillars of rose alabaster up which climbed a vine dense with heavy clusters whose grapes were pearls.
—A Thousand and One Nights

SEDUCTIVE AND SERENE, the romantic bed is one in which you can't help but luxuriate. Whether lavishly outfitted with embroidered sheets, tailored shams, European square pillows, neck-roll pillows, breakfast pillows, gathered bed skirts, and a duvet, or cloistered under an eave and left voluptuously undressed, it beckons with the promise of comfort and seclusion.

Not simply a place for resting or making love, the bed is also a private retreat for musing, sketching, reading, writing, breakfasting, picnicking, and sharing thoughts. It has been the site of some of history's most fateful trysts—whole empires have been born out of the plans conceived in the beds of such seductresses as Cleopatra and Catherine the Great. And one wonders at how many of Napoleon Bonaparte's dreams of glory were dreamed in Josephine's renowned swan bed.

In the days of antiquity, in warm climates, beds were scantily dressed, though seldom without a fine curtain to protect the sleeper from insects. During the following millennium, the bed's foremost feature, like that of most other furniture, was its portability. By the end of the Middle Ages, in areas such as Scotland, Brittany, Scandinavia, and the Greek

A painted cottage-style daybed in the American Empire manner, circa 1900. The carefree setting of the attic hideaway evokes the romance of beach bungalows and summer holidays, when there are hours to indulge in reading romantic novels and writing love letters, **above**.

A colonial mahogany high-post canopy bed from the early nineteenth century with canopy designed by Ronald Bricke & Associates of New York. The Egyptian-style chair dates from the 1920s, **opposite**.

106

A colonial Chippendale-style carved mahogany bed from the early nineteenth century with a flat molded cornice canopy, **below**.

A mahogany lit de repos, **right**, in the Napoleonic manner with Egyptian female head bronze appliques, *circa* 1800. The plush fabric and the scalloped curves of the covering soften the strict angularity of the bed.

islands, wood paneling, or simply three bare walls with a curtain making a fourth, was seen as a satisfactory bunk or cozy sleeping cupboard. In seventeenth-century England and France, the bed grew in significance and grandeur. Some titled figures considered it so prestigious a possession that they bestowed names upon their beds and dressed them in such costumes as "curtains of red velvet, blankets of ermine, and decorations of silver ostrich feathers and leopard heads of gold." Wealthy travelers often carried their favorite beds with them, and the gentry prized them as among the greatest treasures of an estate.

The State Bedchamber became the focus of French court life under Louis XIV, the first king to sleep in state (rather than in a private apartment separate from the state quarters). His bed was equivalent to the throne in terms of the respect it commanded. Like an altar, it was set apart from the rest of the room by a balustrade and was kept sacrosanct under the strict surveillance of a *valet de chambre*. The king received ambassadors and other visitors to the court in his bedchamber, a custom imitated not only in the châteaux of the nobility but also in the salons of the ladies of society, who received social visitors, as well as those bringing congratulations and condolences, while reclining in bed.

Standing high off the floor and draped with two hundred yards of mosquito netting, the nineteenth-century mahogany bed on page 107 floats like an oasis in a room consistently bathed in moonlight. Built in India for a colonial British residence, the bed's height encourages the cooling flow of air around it. The diaphanous veil of fabric, which cascades down the posts and onto the floor from a braid at top, lightens the somber Gothic tone of the room and filters the light that floods in through the undressed windows.

Almost chaste in its formality, a four-poster bed in an Irish castle, page 108, beckons with its old-fashioned simplicity. As modest as a white linen dressing gown, the Chippendale-style bed charms with its naïveté. Pastoral green walls, complemented by the floral pattern on the bed covering, enrich the room's serenity.

*A carved four-poster canopy bed, **left,** in the Italian Renaissance manner with valanced velvet canopy from the early nineteenth century.*

*An English manor-house-style bed with a half canopy with side curtains from the late eighteenth century, **opposite**. The headboard is decorated with the family crest, a fleur-de-lis.*

By way of contrast is the disheveled charm of the English bedroom on page 109, with its passion for home and history. The *lit de repos* that glorifies the intimate studio-like room has been captured in one of the colorful paintings of domestic interiors that hang above it. A note of revelry is implied by the loosely flung velvet bedcovering; its scalloped border evokes the medieval while the bed's Napoleonic air and Egyptian-style *appliques* combine images of empire.

Tones of the Elizabethan era also flavor the more tailored English bedroom on page 110. The scrolled, studded pattern on the hope chest mimics the curves of the canopy, the design of which could have been inspired by Juliet's bodice. The wood of the chest and bed combine beautifully with the blue-greens and deep parchment colors throughout the room.

Regal allusions of a similar time dramatize the sumptuous English bed on page 111. Covered with damasks and adorned with silk fringe and tassels, it speaks of lavish pleasure. A royal crest decorates the headboard, which is crowned with an elaborate canopy whose pewter hue sobers the unvarying brilliance of the room's red, yellow, and blue palette.

A boathouse hideaway is enlivened by the unexpected grandeur of a gilded Swedish Biedermeier canopy bed, at right. The back and one side of the *demi-lune* canopy are draped with folds of "nun's veiling," a wool challis; the other side, with baroque yellow taffeta. The designer chose the two fabrics for their contrasts of crispness and fluidity, transparency and reflectiveness. Making the setting even more luxurious, the pillows, sheets, and bedcoverings are embellished with *soutache*, the intricate braid typically used on French uniforms.

Linda Chase softened the rectilinear monotony of a bedroom in a modern Manhattan apartment building, opposite, by swathing the room in billowing white lace. She framed the period Louis XVI bed with a lace canopy and shirred floor-to-ceiling silk panels trimmed with nineteenth-

A Swedish Biedermeier walnut bed, **above**, with upholstered half-canopy and side curtains (to keep out drafts), from the early nineteenth century, set against a backdrop of crude paneling and plank flooring by designer Ronald Bricke to heighten the effect of elegant surprise. The double ruffle he created at the top of the canopy required fifty yards of taffeta strips. The carved gilded eagle is a symbol of protection.

A period Louis XVI bed with headboard upholstered in silk moiré, **opposite**.

*The subtle combination of off-white curtains and pure white coverings enhances the elegance of the bed, **left**.*

A luxuriously upholstered lit bateau *in the sitting room of fashion designer Jessica McClintock,* **right**.

A French, carved-oak bed with floriated crestrail in the Louis XV manner in Miss McClintock's boudoir, **right**. Laces from her own collection were used in the lavishly feminine canopy.

116

*A Moorish bed set into an arched recess and covered with a gold-embroidered spread, **above**.*

An Italian Renaissance-style lit de repos *in a painted and decorated alcove,* **above**.

century gold braid. The bold stripe of the upholstered headboard serves as a counterpoint to the room's extravagant femininity.

A simple shirred panel dramatizes the head of a bed framed by yards of billowing parchment taffeta, page 114. The antique lace spread and linens clearly express the femininity of its owner.

Pale turquoise hand-painted walls and a crested canopy from which yards of satin are draped contribute to the dreamy classicism of a *lit bateau*, page 115. Located in an upstairs sitting room, it is designed with precise symmetry, more formal in tone than the majestic bed in the boudoir on pages 116 and 117, which is gracefully enveloped in yards and yards of antique fabric. Interior designer Diane Burn designed a half-canopy for this eighteenth-century French bed rather than a full canopy which might have overpowered the ornately carved oak headboard and footboard.

Like romantic mirages, the two Moroccan bedrooms, pages 118 and 119, evoke the "drowsy peace of senses lulled by satiety." Both suggest the splendors of Oriental hospitality and the indolence of a den of contemplation. The dazzlingly elaborate patterning of the wall in the bedroom on 118 is balanced by the gold stripes of the bed covering. In the other, an alcove bed accentuates the aura of retreat in a room saturated with color and visual complexity.

Tropically whimsical, the bed, opposite, is actually a *maquette* for a larger one designed by Mario Villa for a client who wished to indulge a fantasy of sleeping under coconut palms. Villa keeps the model bed in the library of his New Orleans home and uses it as a private oasis. "I love to read and write in bed," he confesses, "and I need to sleep in linen." The Nicaraguan-born designer made the purchase of fine bed linens a personal symbol of his success. "It was one of the first things I bought—not as an extravagance, but because it reminded me of my childhood—of being protected by my mother and father and of returning to my heritage." ॐ

New Orleans designer Mario Villa's Venetian-style coconut-palm bed is an island of quiet in a room that shimmers with a cacophony of textures, **left***.*

Forever enchanting and ageless, dolls represent the ideal: the children we have dreamed of or fondly believe we once were—always charming, eternally playful. Like miniatures, they provide an opportunity for staging an imaginary life—real or fairylike.

Dollhouses were objects of fascination to adults long before they came to occupy the nursery. Tiny, elaborately appointed models were commissioned by ladies and gentlemen of the courts as conversation pieces for the drawing rooms of the seventeenth and eighteenth centuries. Today their appeal is equally as compelling. Colleen Moore, who, as a little girl in the 1920s, inspired her father, a Hollywood set designer, to build her a fairy-tale castle, describes her delight at furnishing this dollhouse with "all the things 'real' people couldn't have....a floor of rose quartz, bordered in green jade, and a solid gold chandelier hung with diamonds and emeralds." ⁊❧

Above, a Victorian lady arrayed in lace and satin looks wistfully toward the garden. Behind her an eighteenth-century French courtesan doll gazes down from inside her gilded frame.

Mirrors of home life, dollhouses range from replications of actual rooms to stages for domestic fantasies. Similarly, dolls offer the opportunity to create scenarios.

A Federal-style dollhouse, **top left**, provides a backdrop in a room occupied by dolls. To the left are antique dolls waiting their turn on stage; at center is a young lady dressed in starched white linen and ready for her recital. **Top right**, a mother prepares to bathe her baby before the fire in a Victorian-style parlor. **Above left**, a group of friends dressed for a masquerade ball prepare to leave an elegant salon on their way to an evening of revelry. **Above right**, a Spanish dancer entertains her sari-clad hostess over tea in a tiny English parlor.

TABLEAUX

I *think of the tableaux in my home as landscapes of objects that delight my eye as much as a painting or sculpture or other piece of fine art.*

—Michael Graves

THE TABLEAU, a picturesque grouping of objects, adds emotional character to an interior by creating a visual story. Almost any type of article—personal mementos, amusing collectibles, works of art, and objects of purely visual fascination, such as fruit, flowers, and shells—can act as a source of inspiration or the starting point for a tableau. Whether simple or elaborate, serious or whimsical, they can be composed anywhere in the home, arranged spontaneously or with great deliberation.

In what could easily be a musician's room, opposite, the display of a bust, a painted portrait, and a photographic portrait create a haunting sense of personal history. The dignity of the faces, their serious presentation (carved in marble and formally framed), and the symmetrical composition give the tableau a feeling of formality, offset by the rustication of the unrestored wooden

*In a setting of Velázquez-like elegance, the tableau, **above**, in Spain has been set for the moment, a composition of spontaneous pleasure.*

chest on which it is arranged. A provincial milk pitcher filled with freshly plucked field flowers adds a note of lyricism and spontaneity. A classical combination of colors—black, deep green, and white—combines with the simple geometry of this tableau's primary shapes—rectangular box and oval frame against a starkly delineated horizontal and vertical backdrop. The overall effect is both highly graphic and traditionally English.

Visually eclectic, but thematically unified, is the bohemian-style tableau arranged by the English designer John Stefanidis in his Dorset country home, overleaf. A carved wooden bust, a line drawing, and a stack of artist's portfolios establish a setting that projects homage to art. Arranged against a white-painted brick wall, the tableau combines the primitive (wicker basket, wooden dish), the exotic (African bust), and the classical (gilt picture frame).

Unlike the previous examples, a tableau can also be composed of homogeneous articles—a collection of coins, for example. To enhance visual interest in what could easily become a monotonous grouping, the coins or other

124

objects can be displayed against a variety of backgrounds—for example, a serious black silk for antique coins, or patriotic red- or green-and-white striped silk for commemorative coins.

A collection of World War I military caps inspired the sentimental tableau, overleaf. The bisque figure in military apparel in the foreground, and the carved gilt wreath, above, add to the feeling of distant memory this composition evokes. The hanging portrait of a woman with a somewhat remote and disapproving, though not mournful, expression lends mystery to the scene—has she lost a son or husband in battle? Compositionally, the "V" neckline of her dress mirrors the shape of the helmets, which is also repeated in the triangle formed by the wire on which the portrait hangs. In keeping with the tableau's military tone, the gold-leaf finish of the picture frame has been dulled to a khaki gold.

A collection of weighty tomes is balanced by the serious expression on the face of the bust in the photo on page 129. Here only three types of objects—books, a bust, and a table—have been used to compose a simple tableau set against a wall whose distressed surface provides an exquisitely colored background. The strength of this arrangement is derived from its proportions; its richness comes from the complex pattern in which the books have been stacked. The marble bust stands out dramatically not only because of its position near center in the symmetrical composition, but because its creamy white color is so prominent a departure from the warmer hues of the books.

*An antique marble bust of a Roman patrician is centered on an antique painted ship-captain's chest in an English home, **preceding page**. The delicate purple flowers had to be vivid enough to stand out against the tableau's dark background.*

*The collection of objects, **left**, reflects the artistic tastes of the English designer John Stefanidis.*

Early-nineteenth-century French and English military officers' helmets create the enigmatic tableau in an English home, **left**. Placed in front and on top of a regiment of old books, the dramatic black-and-gold caps with their bold geometric finials appear almost sculptural.

A tableau composed of a few simple objects is sometimes more difficult to compose than a more complicated arrangement. The simple juxtaposition of a bust and old books against a beautiful distressed wall, **right**, is eloquent in its simplicity.

*An eighteenth-century shagreen néces-
saire with gold studding applied in a
jewel-like manner gives the tableau,
right, an endearing sense of detail.*

Just as the books in the military vignette added to
the scene's sense of history while serving as a backdrop, a shelf
of books provides visual harmony and rhythm to the simple
tableau within a tableau, right. The leather bindings provide an
interesting range of textures, colors, and ornate patterns against
which one small, poetic object stands. Here, a *nécessaire*—a
leather-covered miniature box containing a miniature pencil,
knife, gold spoon, and decanters—was selected for its conver-
sational interest. It stands on an antique *papier mâché* box
whose hand-painted scenic decoration adds pictorial imagery
to the composition.

An eighteenth-century drop-leaf writing desk
serves as a stage for a collection of antique gold and porcelain
boxes, opposite. The symmetry of the piece allows each object
to be presented with equal importance. Accordingly, the larger
papier mâché boxes are centered directly above and below one
another, while the smaller boxes are more randomly placed.
The bronze and gold detailing on the objects corresponds to
the authentic bronze ormolu keyhole mounts on the desk.

Fabric of his own design provides an improvised
backdrop for a "landscape" of objects arranged by the architect
Michael Graves on a Biedermeier secretary, page 132. Graves,
who is known for his affection for the classical and the quirky,
likes to collect and arrange pieces of ivory, drafting instru-
ments, nineteenth and twentieth-century recreations of Pompeian artifacts made by French, Italian, and English
craftsmen, and neoclassical picture frames and magnifying
glasses.

*Assorted Victorian porcelain and
opaline boxes are arranged on a coun-
try-French fruitwood desk cabinet,
opposite.*

Linda Chase used her living room desk as the stage for a highly feminine tableau shown on the following pages. Although many of the items, such as the traveling lap desk and the antique Indian calligraphy set, might be found on any writing table, the designer has surrounded herself with romantic objects as sources of inspiration for her work and her thoughts. For example, a painted scene of troubadours singing of love combines with painted miniatures of ladies-in-waiting from the French courts and a jeweled miniature of an Arabian knight. A whimsical topiary draped with dried rosebuds further evokes the ambience of the French court. The flowers are reflected in the painting that hangs above, a dreamy scene in which one woman plucks roses from a garden, eavesdropping, perhaps, while two lovers nearby share a secret. Together, all the figures in this tableau—from desk to painting to the eighteenth-century French *automate* of Mozart in the foreground—are spinning a fantasy for the romantic imagination.

In an even more intricate tableau, page 136, a collage of highly detailed antique pieces has been arranged on an ornately patterned eighteenth-century hand-painted Italian desk. Though they appear randomly placed, the objects have been organized around the early-eighteenth-century French clock adorned with hand-painted scenes and bronze ormolu mountings. The composition is tied together by the overall decorativeness of all the pieces. To evoke the Old World, an antique painting with fanciful European imagery was hung above the tableau. The muted colors in the painting repeat those of the objects on the table, and its size and proportions complement those of the tableau. In addition, the antique gold-leaf frame mirrors the ormolu on the writing table.

An uninhibited lack of artifice gives a tableau set in an Irish castle, page 137, its naive charm. The cracked plaster finish on the white-painted walls provides a hauntingly austere backdrop for this rhapsodic little arrangement of

*A tableau composed by the architect Michael Graves, **left**, is made dramatic by the combination of black and white pieces on the satinwood surface of a Biedermeier secretary.*

133

paintings and porcelains. A romantic portrait of Olivia from Shakespeare's *Twelfth Night*, framed in gold, hangs above a symmetrical ensemble of continental porcelains, all of which are embellished with wistful *putti* and female figures. The tilt of the candlesticks, one of which is more than slightly skewed, adds a note of unexpected animation to what might otherwise be a stiffly formal and far less interesting tableau.

Silver serving pieces arranged in two separate tableaux add elegance and light to the comfortable English dining room, pages 138 and 139. The simple but formal grouping at the center of the dining table is enlivened by a casual bouquet of lilacs. The collection of large polished and unpolished pieces, massed on the sideboard at left, returns the light entering the room from a window opposite back across the table in a blanket of reflection. The elaborately detailed silver in both tableaux mirrors the intricacy of the ceiling pattern and the ornateness of the gilded frames on the portraits that border the room.

A miniature writing desk, page 140, provides an enchanting stage for a collection of hand-painted porcelain miniatures as well as other precious objects of personal meaning to Linda Chase. The designer mixed framed porcelain miniatures with others mounted in bronze and gold boxes and lined in velvet. These boxes were originally intended to hold objects of whim, such as rings, pins, or even snuff. Miss Chase placed an antique French royal napkin ring, a keepsake prized for its personal and historical value, at center stage, and added a miniature vitrine of flowers, doll-like in proportion, just as she would have placed a bouquet atop her larger living room desk.

A period French boulliotte *lamp's shape reflects the shape of the hand-painted scrolls on the wall of Linda Chase's New York apartment,* **left**. *In the foreground, an eighteenth-century French* automate *of Mozart composes by candlelight.*

The rich combination of a great number of highly detailed antique pieces gives the tableau, **left**, its jeweled look. The contrast of the rough-textured wall behind accentuates the delicacy of the continental treasures. Although allowed to remain in its slightly worn condition, the table was given the fanciful addition of a tassel on its key.

Antique white Meissen candelabra animate an Irish drawing room, **opposite**. An antique brass and glass wall-mounted candle holder interjects a note of compositional surprise to the tableau, set in an Irish castle.

A softly feminine tableau centers around the bust of a young girl, page 141. Sheer fabrics and an arrangement of wispy baby's breath and roses complement the figure's delicacy. A variety of hard-edged objects—silver mirror, crystal box, wrought-iron frame—prevent the visual tone from becoming saccharine. The palette—white with black accents—intensifies the drama of the tableau. The pearls, in particular, displayed in a black-and-white dish, echo the colors of the background and the femininity and elegance of the scene.

Equally feminine, yet strongly classical, is the simple tableau, page 142, composed of four intricately detailed pieces. In the right foreground, an antique Baccarat crystal and *doré* bronze box holds a bouquet of full-blooming roses. The roses have been arranged rectangularly, reiterating the shape of the container and that of the painting behind it. Soft, ephemeral, and bright in color, they also provide contrast with the worn antique frame, on which the aged gold has oxidized, producing a beautiful, mottled, putty-green color. Throughout the tableau, gold detailing keeps the eye moving among the objects. The gold inner line of the frame, for example, repeats the gold border and keymount of the Baccarat box and is also reflected in the two rams' heads and painted gold patterning of the eighteenth-century French Sèvres urn. Surrounding the urn's lid is a white porcelain detailed band with gold highlights that also closely resembles the outer band on the painting's frame.

The geometric composition of the tableau is accentuated by the column-like period English candlestick, embellished with scrolls and garlands. Its silver finish also

*The grouping of assorted Victorian silver-plated articles in the tableau, **right**, includes a sugar bowl, footed biscuit jar, footed round tea tray in the Chippendale manner, and a pair of candelabra.*

adds sparkle to the tableau just as the fine lace and antique table linens add softness.

The highly architectural quality of the setting on page 143 is offset by the sweeping curvilinear grace of the antique Italian dressing table just as the table's hand-painted top offsets the hard edges of the beveled wrought-iron mirror above it. The colors on the table's surface are reminiscent of an Italian landscape. The scallop motif is Pompeian in feeling. The tableau consists of a number of elegantly romantic objects—crystal and silver decanters, antique silver hairbrush, lace handkerchiefs, perfume bottles, and *shagreen* boxes, all of which reflect the refined tastes of their owner.

In the Los Angeles kitchen, page 144, an antique English bird cage of weathered wood sets the tone for a tableau that invites the garden indoors. The whimsical cage is crowned with a domed top that offers a pleasing contrast to the geometric shapes of the kitchen panels. The geometry of the copper chocolate service also reflects that of the kitchen's interior. Less formal than sterling or gold plate, the copper mixes naturally with the room's terra cotta detailing and earthy atmosphere.

On the opposite side of the kitchen, fine linen, porcelain, and lace express the quintessence of romance. Linda Chase framed the vignette in flowers: potted snapdragons arranged in antique English knife boxes, below, and a bower of fresh roses and zinnias, above, which were first bound with hemp into small bouquets and then hung from a trellis to dry. Like the open door of the bird cage, the vine growing in through the window extends the tableau's invitation to nature.

*The tableau, **opposite**, composed by interior designer Diane Burn incorporates classical expressions of luxury and femininity.*

*The cabinetmaker's sample of a sécretaire abattant, **above**, was made for a client by an eighteenth-century craftsman to illustrate exactly what the actual piece of furniture would look like. Exquisitely detailed down to the handmade bronze ormolu hardware and fittings, this intricate replica makes an ideal setting for a tableau composed of miniatures.*

Linda Chase's elegant grouping, **opposite**, includes a Louis XV decorated porcelain urn with gilt ram's-head handles, an Adam silver candlestick, and a cut-crystal Baccarat box. The murky quality of the landscape painting exudes a gentleness that enhances the beauty of the roses below it.

The surface of the antique Italian dressing table, **left**, was hand-painted in a palette that matches the rosa alacante marble wainscoting behind it. Peonies and lace were chosen to soften the linear classicism of the tableau.

143

The sweet and simple face of the early-eighteenth-century French clock, **below left**, balances the complexity of the composition below it. The table setting mixes French Empire chocolate cups with Meissen chocolate and coffee cups and Waterford stemware.

An antique English coffee service was grouped with an antique French wire-and-wood bird cage to emphasize the provincial look of the kitchen, **above**.

Potato and spinach croquettes

*The humble, indispensable potato is enhanced with the flavours of spinach
and Parmesan in these popular delights.*

Preparation time **30 minutes**
Total cooking time **45 minutes**
Makes 14 croquettes

500 g (1 lb) floury potatoes
pinch of ground nutmeg
20 g (3/4 oz) unsalted butter
1 egg yolk
oil, for deep- or shallow-frying
40 g (1 1/4 oz) Parmesan, freshly grated
50 g (1 3/4 oz) cooked English spinach, finely chopped
60 g (2 oz) plain flour, seasoned with salt and pepper
3 eggs, beaten
1 tablespoon peanut (groundnut) oil
150 g (5 oz) dry breadcrumbs

1 Cut the potatoes into similar-sized pieces for even cooking, by halving or quartering, depending on their size. Put in a saucepan, cover with cold water and add a large pinch of salt. Bring to the boil, lower the heat and cook for at least 20 minutes, or until quite tender.

2 Drain the potatoes and dry them by shaking them in the pan over low heat for 2 minutes. Press them through a sieve or finely mash them until smooth. Season with salt and pepper, to taste, and nutmeg. Add the butter and egg yolk. Spread out on a tray to cool. Preheat oil in a deep-fryer or large pan, to moderate 180°C (350°F). The oil will be hot enough when a cube of bread browns in 15 seconds.

3 Mix the Parmesan with the very well-drained spinach in a bowl. Add the potato, salt and pepper to this mixture and stir to combine. On a floured surface, and using floured hands, roll the mixture beneath a flat hand to form cylinders about 6 x 2 cm (2 1/2 x 3/4 inches). Even up and flatten the ends.

4 Place the seasoned flour on a tray. Combine the eggs and oil in a bowl and put the breadcrumbs on a large piece of greaseproof paper. Roll the croquettes carefully through the flour and pat off the excess. Dip them in the egg to coat thoroughly, drain off the excess and roll in the breadcrumbs, lifting the edges of the paper to make it easier. Sometimes it is necessary to coat the croquettes twice in the egg and crumbs. Do this if your mixture is a little too soft to hold its shape well. Fry in batches until evenly browned and lift out, shaking off any excess oil. Drain on crumpled paper towels.

Chef's tips The potato must not be too wet as the croquettes will split and absorb the oil.

Shake off or press on excess breadcrumbs or they will burn and cling to the croquettes as unsightly specks.

Mediterranean-style roasted capsicums

This colourful, tasty dish is suitable for serving as a first course or using as a side dish with seafood, meat or chicken.

*Preparation time **10 minutes** + **3–4 hours marinating***
*Total cooking time **10–15 minutes***
Serves 6

1 red capsicum (pepper)
1 green capsicum (pepper)
1 yellow capsicum (pepper)
2 teaspoons capers, finely chopped
4 anchovy fillets, finely chopped
3 tablespoons fresh basil leaves, shredded
80 ml (2³/4 fl oz) olive oil

1 Cut all the capsicums in half, remove the seeds and membranes and put the cut capsicums on a grill tray cut-side-down.
2 Brush the capsicums with a little oil and cook under a preheated grill until the skin has blackened and blistered. Cover with a tea towel or enclose in a plastic bag and allow the capsicums to cool. The skins will then come away from the flesh more easily.
3 Remove the skins, cut the flesh into thick strips and put them in a bowl.
4 Place the capers, anchovies and basil in a jug, stir in the olive oil and pour the mixture over the capsicums. Season, to taste, with salt and pepper. Marinate in the refrigerator for 3–4 hours before serving. Serve with focaccia and a green salad.

Eggplant caviar

The name of this dish comes from the rather grainy appearance of the eggplant.
Delicious served with crisp Melba toast or warmed pitta bread.

*Preparation time **10 minutes + 1 hour refrigeration***
*Total cooking time **30 minutes***
Serves 6

800 g (1 lb 10 oz) eggplants (aubergines)
50 g (1³/4 oz) pitted black olives, chopped
1 clove garlic, crushed
4 tablespoons finely chopped fresh chives
155 ml (5 fl oz) olive oil
¹/2 teaspoon paprika

1   Preheat the oven to moderate 180°C (350°F/Gas 4).
Cut the eggplants in half lengthways. Brush the cut sides
with a little olive oil and sprinkle with salt and pepper.

Bake for 25–30 minutes, or until the flesh is very soft.
2   Drain the eggplants to remove any liquid. Scrape out
the flesh with a spoon, chop the flesh and put in a bowl.
3   Add the black olives, garlic and half the chives. Mix
everything together using a fork, squeezing the eggplant
flesh against the sides of the bowl to break it down. Add
the olive oil very slowly, stirring it into the mixture with
the fork. Add the paprika and season, to taste, with salt
and pepper. Refrigerate for 1 hour.
4   Spoon into a chilled bowl, sprinkle the top with the
reserved chives and serve with Melba toast.

Chef's tip For a special presentation, use two spoons to
shape the mixture into small quenelles and arrange on
individual plates. Sprinkle with chopped chives.

Braised red cabbage

The French name for this northern dish, an excellent accompaniment to roast pork or game, is Chou rouge à la flamande. Slow-cooking produces a wonderful result.

Preparation time **20 minutes**
Total cooking time **1 hour 45 minutes**
Serves 8

1 red cabbage
45 g (1¹/₂ oz) unsalted butter
1 onion, sliced
2 cooking apples
2 tablespoons white wine vinegar
1 tablespoon sugar
1¹/₂ tablespoons plain flour

1 Preheat the oven to warm 170°C (325°F/Gas 3). Quarter the cabbage, cut out and discard the stalk and shred the cabbage finely. Put the cabbage in a large saucepan of boiling salted water (there should be enough water to more than cover the cabbage), bring back to the boil and drain. The cabbage will now have taken on an inky blue colour. This is normal, and it will regain its colour later. You may have to do this in batches, depending on the size of the saucepan.

2 Melt 15 g (¹/₂ oz) of the butter in a large casserole, add the onion, cover and cook gently until transparent. Peel, quarter, core and slice the apples finely before adding them to the onion. Cook for a few minutes, remove the mixture from the dish and set aside.

3 Add the cabbage to the casserole, layering with the onion and apple mixture and sprinkling with the vinegar, sugar and 2 tablespoons of water. Season with salt and pepper. You will see the red colour return as the vinegar is added. Cover with thickly buttered paper and the lid and bake for about 1¹/₂ hours, or until very tender. Stir occasionally and moisten with a little extra water if necessary.

4 Soften the remaining butter in a bowl and mix in the flour. Push the cabbage to one side of the pan. There will be some liquid at the bottom of the casserole. Add one quarter of the butter and flour and stir in. The liquid will thicken slightly. Repeat on the other side. Toss together and only add more butter and flour if any watery liquid is present. A lot of flavour and seasoning is in the liquid, so it is just thickened to cling to the cabbage. Do not thicken too much. Taste and season. The cabbage should be gently sweet and sour. It may be necessary to add a little more sugar or vinegar, to taste.

Little stuffed vegetables

*Master the preparation of these delightful, elegant vegetables so you and
your friends can savour the results.*

*Preparation time **45 minutes***
*Total cooking time **1 hour***
Serves 4

125 g (4 oz) fresh breadcrumbs
170 ml (5¹/2 fl oz) milk
olive oil, for cooking
125 g (4 oz) lean pork, minced
125 g (4 oz) lean veal, minced
3 cloves garlic, finely chopped
1 egg yolk, lightly beaten
2 tablespoons chopped fresh parsley
4 small turnips, about 5 cm (2 inches)
   in diameter
1 large zucchini (courgette), at least 21 cm
   (8¹/2 inches) in length, ends removed
2 large potatoes, peeled

1 Preheat the oven to moderately hot 200°C (400°F/
Gas 6). Mix the breadcrumbs and milk in a large bowl
and set aside while you cook the meat. In a large frying
pan, heat a little olive oil and cook the pork, veal and
garlic for 5 minutes over medium heat. Remove from

the heat and mix into the bread and milk. Season, to
taste, and add the egg and parsley. Set aside.

2 Peel the turnips and slice off the tops and bottoms,
leaving the vegetables 4 cm (1¹/2 inches) high with a
4–5 cm (1¹/2–2 inch) diameter. Use a melon baller to
scoop the flesh out. Discard the flesh, leaving a border
1 cm (1/2 inch) thick on the sides and bottom. Cut the
zucchini into lengths, about 4 cm (1¹/2 inches) each,
and scoop the flesh out, as with the turnips.

3 Cut the potatoes into 4 cm (1¹/2 inch) cubes and,
using a 4 cm (1¹/2 inch) round cutter, cut the potatoes
into round tubes. Scoop out the centre as for the other
vegetables. Blanch each vegetable in a separate pan of
boiling water, being careful not to overcook any of
them. They should remain firm. Transfer the turnips and
zucchini to a bowl of iced water and, when completely
cooled, place upside down on paper towels to drain.
When the potatoes are cooked, put them on paper
towels, right-side-up, until cool enough to handle.

4 Season the interiors of the prepared vegetables and
spoon the filling into them. Place the filled vegetables in
a lightly oiled ovenproof dish and brush with a little
olive oil. Bake for 20–30 minutes, or until just tender. If
desired, brown under a grill. Serve hot or cold.

Vegetable strudel

A delightful start to a meal or perfect as a light luncheon dish. A slight hint of curry flavour enhances the lightly cooked vegetables in crisp pastry.

Preparation time **40 minutes**
Total cooking time **1 hour**
Serves 4–6 (Makes 10)

oil, for cooking
1 onion, chopped
1/2 teaspoon mild curry powder
450 g (14 1/4 oz) mixed peeled vegetables,
  such as finely diced carrot, parsnip, turnip
  and celeriac; French beans, cut into short
  lengths; one quarter each of a cauliflower
  and a broccoli, cut into tiny florets; a small
  leek, finely sliced (see page 63)
2 tablespoons fresh breadcrumbs
20 sheets filo pastry
oil or melted butter, for brushing

TOMATO AND CORIANDER SAUCE
15 g (1/2 oz) unsalted butter
1 onion, finely sliced
450 g (14 1/4 oz) tomatoes, peeled, seeded and
  quartered (see page 62)
  or 400 g (12 3/4 oz) can tomatoes
60 ml (2 fl oz) vegetable or chicken stock
  (see page 63)
1 bay leaf
1 sprig of fresh thyme
3 tablespoons chopped fresh coriander leaves

1 Preheat the oven to moderately hot 190°C (375°F/ Gas 5). Heat a little oil in a sauté pan or wok and gently fry the onion until just soft. Add the curry powder and blend in. Add the carrot, parsnip, turnip and celeriac and toss for 2 minutes over high heat. Add the beans, cauliflower and leek and toss for another minute before adding the broccoli and frying for 2 minutes. Transfer to a large bowl, lightly mix in the breadcrumbs and season with salt and pepper, to taste.

2 Brush one sheet of filo pastry with oil or melted butter and place another sheet on top before brushing again with oil or melted butter. Fold in half and scatter on the vegetables, leaving 2.5 cm (1 inch) on each side free of filling. Turn these sides in and roll up the strudel carefully. Repeat this process until all the filo pastry and vegetables have been used. Transfer the strudels to a lightly buttered baking tray and gently brush the pastry with oil or melted butter. Bake for 15–20 minutes, or until crisp and golden brown.

3 To make the tomato and coriander sauce, melt the butter in a pan, add the onion and cook for 10 minutes until transparent. Add the tomato, stock, bay leaf and thyme, and season with salt and pepper. Bring to the boil, reduce the heat, cover and simmer for up to 20 minutes, or until rich and pulpy. (If using canned tomatoes, add with the juice and, when soft, remove the lid and cook to reduce until thick.) Remove from the heat. Discard the bay leaf and thyme, add the coriander and season, to taste. A pinch of sugar may be required if the tomatoes are sharp. Serve the strudels immediately with the tomato and coriander sauce.

Chef's tips The strudels should be served as soon as they are cooked, otherwise the pastry may go soft. If you prefer, prepare the strudels a few hours ahead and brush again with melted butter just before baking.

This is an excellent recipe to use up small amounts of fresh vegetables in your refrigerator. Be careful not to use vegetables that will become watery and make the pastry soggy, such as zucchini (courgettes). If using up cooked vegetables, dice them and mix in after cooking the onion, but do not cook further.

Roasted parsnips with honey and ginger

A very popular vegetable in Ancient Greece and during the Middle Ages and the Renaissance, the parsnip has a lovely sweet flavour.

Preparation time **10 minutes**
Total cooking time **20 minutes**
Serves 6

6 parsnips, about 750 g (1¹/₂ lb)
60 ml (2 fl oz) oil
15 g (¹/₂ oz) unsalted butter
1 tablespoon clear honey
1 tablespoon finely grated or chopped fresh ginger

1 Preheat the oven to hot 220°C (425°F/Gas 7). Cut the peeled parsnips in half lengthways, or quarters if they are large, to make pieces about 8 cm (3 inches) long and 2.5 cm (1 inch) thick. Remove any woody cores. Put in a large pan and cover with water. Add a pinch of salt and bring to the boil over high heat. Boil for 1 minute before draining. Return to the saucepan and dry well by shaking the pan over low heat for about 1 minute.

2 Heat the oil in a roasting pan on the stove. Add the parsnips and cook quickly over high heat, turning to colour evenly. Add the butter to the pan, transfer to the oven for 10 minutes. Spoon or tip out the excess oil.

3 Add the honey and ginger, turning the parsnips to coat evenly, and roast for another 5 minutes.

4 Lift the parsnips out of the pan and serve hot with pork or chicken.

Baked eggplant

The pronounced flavour of the eggplant is often combined with tomato, garlic and herbs.
These stuffed eggplants originated in Turkey as Imam bayildi.

Preparation time **40 minutes**
Total cooking time **1 hour**
Serves 4

olive oil, for cooking
2 large French shallots, finely chopped
800 g (1 lb 10 oz) tomatoes, peeled, seeded
  and diced (see page 62)
6 cloves garlic, finely chopped
small pinch of cayenne pepper
60 g (2 oz) fresh basil leaves, chopped
2 small eggplants (aubergines)
4 small tomatoes, stems removed
100 g (3¼ oz) Gruyère or Swiss cheese, grated

1 Preheat the oven to slow 150°C (300°F/Gas 2). In a heavy-based frying pan, heat a little oil over medium heat, add the shallots and cook for 2–3 minutes, without colouring. Add the diced tomato and garlic, season with salt and cayenne pepper and simmer for 15 minutes, or until thick. Mix in the chopped basil, set aside and keep warm.

2 Meanwhile, cut the eggplants in half lengthways. Score the flesh, being careful not to cut through the skin. Rub the surface with olive oil and season with salt. Place the eggplant cut-side-down in an ovenproof dish or roasting pan and bake for 15 minutes, or until soft. Allow to cool. Increase the temperature of the oven to moderately hot 200°C (400°F/Gas 6).

3 Cut the small tomatoes in half from top to bottom and thinly slice into semicircles. Set aside.

4 Carefully scoop out the flesh of the cooked eggplant. Set the empty skins aside. Chop up the pulp and remove some of the liquid by cooking in a frying pan for 5–10 minutes over low heat. Transfer the eggplant pulp to a bowl and mix in half of the cooked tomato. Season and then spoon the mixture into the eggplant skins. Put the filled eggplants in an ovenproof dish and arrange the tomato slices on top. Sprinkle with the grated cheese and bake until golden brown.

5 Purée the remaining cooked tomato in a blender. Thin out if necessary with some water or chicken stock. Place in a small saucepan and heat through, checking the seasoning. To serve, spoon some of the tomato sauce onto the plate and arrange the eggplant on top.

Cauliflower cheese

Perfect partners, cauliflower and cheese baked in this way make a hearty winter dish that never has the experience of being a leftover.

*Preparation time **10 minutes***
*Total cooking time **30 minutes***
Serves 4–6

1 whole cauliflower, about 470 g (15 oz)
  when trimmed
30 g (1 oz) unsalted butter
30 g (1 oz) plain flour
500 ml (16 fl oz) milk
pinch of ground nutmeg
100 ml (3 1/4 fl oz) cream
130 g (4 1/4 oz) Gruyère cheese, grated
2 egg yolks

1 Preheat the oven to moderate 180°C (350°F/Gas 4). Remove the outer leaves of the cauliflower and break the head into small serving-sized pieces. Place in cold salted water, bring slowly to the boil, reduce the heat and simmer for about 10 minutes, or until the cauliflower is cooked, but still slightly firm. Drain, refresh in cold water, then drain again.

2 To make the cheese sauce, melt the butter in a pan, stir in the flour with a wooden spoon or whisk and cook over low heat for 3 minutes. Remove from the heat and gradually stir in the cold milk. Return to the heat and bring to the boil, stirring continuously. Add the nutmeg and season with salt and pepper. Stir in the cream. Remove from the heat and add 100 g (3 1/4 oz) of cheese and the egg yolks. Set aside. Cover the surface with plastic wrap or damp greaseproof paper to prevent a skin from forming.

3 Lightly brush an ovenproof dish with butter. Pour a thin layer of the sauce onto the base, arrange the cauliflower on the sauce and pour over the remaining sauce so that it coats the cauliflower. Sprinkle with the remaining cheese and some pepper and nutmeg and bake for 15 minutes, or until the cheese is golden brown.

Chef's tips If the sauce looks lumpy before the cream has been added to it, simply whisk it until smooth. It is important to do this before the cheese is added to prevent strands of cheese from sticking to the whisk.

Gruyère is a strong cheese, but if you use a different type with less strength, add a little mustard to bring out the flavours.

Asparagus with hollandaise sauce

Before World War I, hollandaise sauce was called Sauce Isigny, after a town in Normandy known for its butter. During the war, butter production came to a halt and it was imported from Holland. The name was changed to hollandaise to indicate the source of the butter and was never changed back.

*Preparation time **45 minutes***
*Total cooking time **35 minutes***
Serves 4

HOLLANDAISE SAUCE
3 egg yolks
200 g (6¹/₂ oz) clarified butter, melted
  (see page 63)
small pinch of cayenne pepper
juice of ¹/₂ lemon

32 asparagus spears
4 tablespoons rock salt

1 To make the hollandaise sauce, whisk the egg yolks with 3 tablespoons of water in a medium heatproof bowl until foamy. Put the bowl over a larger pan of simmering water and continue whisking over low heat until the mixture is thick and you can see the trail made by the whisk. Remove from the heat and gradually add the butter, whisking constantly. Once all the butter has been incorporated, strain the sauce and season with salt, to taste, a dash of cayenne pepper and the lemon juice. Keep the sauce warm over a pan of warm water. (If preferred, a food processor can be used to make the sauce. Whisk the egg yolks and water and, with the motor running, add the melted warm butter to the processor in a thin stream.)

2 Bring a large pan of water to the boil. Use a vegetable peeler to remove the outer layer from the lower two thirds of the stem of each asparagus spear. Line up the spears of asparagus and tie into bundles of eight.

3 Add the rock salt and then the asparagus bundles to the water. Reduce the heat and simmer for 10 minutes, or until the tips are tender. Remove and drain on paper towels. Remove the string and arrange each bundle on a warm plate. Coat with some of the hollandaise sauce and serve immediately.

Chef's tip Hollandaise sauce is an emulsion sauce like mayonnaise, but made with warm clarified butter, which helps to make a smooth sauce. Once made, the sauce should be kept lukewarm. If the sauce is overheated, it will separate. If this should happen, the sauce can be repaired by adding a little cold water and whisking.

Ratatouille

This is a classic dish from the sunny area of Provence using the freshest tomatoes, zucchini, eggplants, capsicums and onions, sautéed in olive oil with herbs.

*Preparation time **40 minutes***
*Total cooking time **1 hour***
Serves 4

1 onion, diced
80 ml (2³/4 fl oz) olive oil, for cooking
250 g (8 oz) tomatoes, peeled, seeded
 and chopped (see page 62)
2 cloves garlic, chopped
1 red capsicum (pepper), seeded and cut
 into short strips
bouquet garni (see Chef's tips)
250 g (8 oz) zucchini (courgettes), cut
 into batons (see page 63)
250 g (8 oz) eggplants (aubergines), cut
 into batons
60 g (2 oz) chopped fresh basil leaves

1 Preheat the oven to moderate 180°C (350°F/Gas 4). In an ovenproof frying pan, cook the onion in a little of the olive oil, over medium-low heat, for 3–5 minutes, or until soft, being careful not to let the onion colour. Add the tomato and garlic and cook for 15 minutes, stirring occasionally.

2 In another frying pan, sauté the red capsicum in oil for 2–3 minutes over medium-high heat. Strain off the excess oil and add to the tomato mixture with the bouquet garni.

3 Sauté the prepared zucchini and eggplant separately in oil, for 3–4 minutes. Add to the tomato mixture. Season with salt and pepper, to taste, cover and bake for 30 minutes. Just before serving, remove the bouquet garni, stir in the chopped fresh basil leaves and adjust the seasoning, if necessary.

Chef's tips The bouquet garni is a selection of herbs tied in a neat bundle for easy removal from the dish before serving. It is made by wrapping the green part of a leek around celery leaves, a sprig of thyme, a bay leaf and parsley stalks, and then securing them together with string. When using a herb such as basil in the recipe, you can replace the parsley stalks with the basil stalks for added flavour.

This dish can be made on the stove top instead of being baked. Cook over low heat, stirring often.

Provençal stuffed tomatoes

Olive oil, garlic, parsley and tomato predominate in the cuisine of the Provence region, reflecting its close proximity to Italy.

Preparation time **30 minutes + 20 minutes draining**
Total cooking time **15 minutes**
Serves 4

4 tomatoes
60 ml (2 fl oz) extra virgin olive oil
4 cloves garlic, finely chopped
1 tablespoon chopped fresh thyme leaves
2 tablespoons chopped fresh parsley
60 g (2 oz) fresh breadcrumbs

1 Preheat the oven to moderately hot 190°C (375°F/Gas 5). Remove the stem ends from the tomatoes. Place the tomatoes stem-side-down (to make the tomatoes more secure) and cut in half. Carefully remove the seeds with a teaspoon. Season with some salt and leave, cut-side-down, on paper towels to drain for about 20 minutes.

2 Gently heat the olive oil until warm. Remove from the heat and add the garlic, thyme, parsley and breadcrumbs. Season with salt and pepper and mix well using a wooden spoon. Season the tomato halves with pepper and fill with the bread stuffing, making a slight dome on top of each tomato half. Place in an oiled ovenproof dish and drizzle with some extra olive oil. Bake for 5–10 minutes, or until the stuffing is golden.

Chef's tip This recipe would also work successfully using eight small tomatoes with the tops cut off and the seeds scooped out.

Mixed glazed vegetables

This colourful, attractively prepared mixture of vegetables looks very appealing presented at the table in a shallow dish.

Preparation time **40 minutes**
Total cooking time **30 minutes**
Serves 4

20 pearl onions
2 zucchini (courgettes)
3 turnips
3 carrots
60 g (2 oz) unsalted butter
3 teaspoons sugar

1 Soak the pearl onions in a bowl of warm water for 5 minutes, to make peeling easier. Lightly trim the root end, being careful not to cut off too much, since it is the root end that will keep the pearl onions intact.

2 Using a standard 2 cm (3/4 inch) melon baller, make 20 balls each of the zucchini, turnip and carrot. Cook the zucchini balls for 1 minute in boiling salted water and refresh in iced water. Drain and transfer to a small saucepan. Add one third of the butter, 1 teaspoon of the sugar, 1/2 teaspoon salt and 30 ml (1 fl oz) water and cook until the water has evaporated and a syrupy glaze remains. Check to see if the vegetables are tender. If not, add some water and cook a little longer. Roll the vegetables around to evenly coat, then set aside and keep warm.

3 Put the turnip and carrot balls together in a pan with half of the remaining butter, 1 teaspoon of the sugar, 1/2 teaspoon salt and enough water to just cover. Cook in the same way as the zucchini, then set aside and keep warm. Repeat with the peeled pearl onions.

4 Reheat by combining the vegetables in a pan, placing the pan over medium heat and rolling the vegetables around to prevent them from browning, for about 3–5 minutes. Transfer to a serving dish.

Chef's tips Leave the vegetables at room temperature for about 1 hour before preparing.

If you can't get pearl onions, use small pickling onions and remove a few outer layers.

Chickpea and sesame fritters with garlic and olive sauce

Chickpeas feature in many dishes in the south of France, as well as in the Middle East and Spain.
These fritters team well with the garlicky flavour of the sauce.

*Preparation time **55 minutes + 30 minutes soaking***
*Total cooking time **2 hours***
Makes 20

170 g (5¹/² oz) dried chickpeas
80 ml (2³/4 fl oz) sesame oil
2 eggs, beaten
125 g (4 oz) sesame seeds
oil, for deep-frying

GARLIC AND OLIVE SAUCE
¹/² head of garlic, separated into cloves
  and peeled
15 g (¹/² oz) unsalted butter
¹/² onion, chopped
200 ml (6¹/² fl oz) milk
50 ml (1³/4 fl oz) cream, optional
100 g (3¹/4 oz) black olives, chopped

1 tablespoon chopped fresh flat-leaf parsley or
  fresh coriander leaves, optional

1 Soak the chickpeas in warm water for 30 minutes. Drain, cover well with fresh water in a deep pan and simmer for about 1¹/2 hours, or until soft.

2 Drain the chickpeas and while hot, purée them in a food processor until fine. Slowly incorporate the sesame oil. Season with salt and pepper, to taste.

3 Roll the mixture into balls about the size of a dessertspoon. Dip them in the beaten egg and coat with the sesame seeds. Heat the oil to moderate 180°C (350°F), and deep-fry the balls in batches until golden. Drain on paper towels and keep warm.

4 To make the garlic and olive sauce, gently sauté the garlic in the butter until golden brown. Add the onion and cook until the onion is just soft but without colour. Add the milk, bring to the boil and cook for 10 minutes. Purée the mixture in a blender, add the cream, and salt and pepper, to taste. Strain the sauce and add the chopped black olives.

5 Place three or four of the chickpea fritters per person on plates and pour the garlic and olive sauce around them. Sprinkle with the chopped fresh parsley or coriander leaves and serve immediately.

Vegetable tian

Layers of vegetables with added flavour from herbs and garlic are delicious baked in a shallow dish that can be presented at the table. Suitable for lunch or dinner.

*Preparation time **30 minutes***
*Total cooking time **1 hour***
Serves 4

olive oil, for cooking
1 small onion, thinly sliced
750 g (1½ lb) tomatoes, peeled, seeded
  and diced (see page 62)
400 g (12¾ oz) large mushrooms, thinly sliced
400 g (12¾ oz) potatoes, thinly sliced
2 cloves garlic, finely chopped
500 g (1 lb) English spinach leaves,
  stems removed
1 sprig of fresh rosemary
3 tablespoons chopped fresh parsley

1 Preheat the oven to moderately hot 190°C (375°F/Gas 5). In a heavy-based pan, heat a little olive oil over medium heat and gently cook the sliced onion with a pinch of salt for 3 minutes, without allowing to colour. Add the seeded and diced tomato and cook gently for 7 minutes. Season, to taste, and set aside.

2 Pan-fry the mushrooms in a little olive oil over high heat for 3–4 minutes. Drain off any excess moisture. Season, to taste, and set aside.

3 Pan-fry the potato in batches in some olive oil, over medium-low heat for 3 minutes. Return all the potato to the pan, add the garlic and cook for another minute. Season with salt and freshly ground black pepper and drain on paper towels.

4 Arrange a layer of potato in the bottom of a 2-litre capacity, 20 cm (8 inch) diameter round or oval ovenproof dish and cover with a layer of the mushrooms followed by a layer of spinach, then tomato. Bake for 30–45 minutes, covered with greaseproof paper. Sprinkle with rosemary leaves and parsley before serving.

Chef's tip If desired, cover the vegetables with grated Parmesan or crumbled feta cheese before baking.

Celeriac rémoulade

This is a delicious first course or can be served as a light lunch, perhaps with chunks of bread.
The mustardy mayonnaise enhances the crunchy celeriac's unique taste.

*Preparation time **40 minutes***
  *+ **30–60 minutes** resting*
*Total cooking time **Nil***
Serves 4–6

2–3 celeriac, total weight about 1.3 kg (2 lb 10 oz)
juice of 1 lemon
several small salad leaves, to garnish
2 tomatoes, peeled, seeded and diced
  (see page 62), to garnish
walnut halves, to garnish

REMOULADE SAUCE
2 egg yolks
2 tablespoons Dijon mustard
pinch of cayenne pepper
250 ml (8 fl oz) peanut (groundnut) oil

1 Using a large knife, cut each celeriac in half and peel away the skin, cutting about 3 mm (1/8 inch) deep under the skin (the skin is very fibrous so it is important to cut off enough). Coarsely grate the celeriac and put the flesh in a bowl. Season with salt and pepper and toss in the lemon juice. Cover with plastic wrap and set aside for 30–60 minutes.

2 To make the rémoulade sauce, in a medium bowl, whisk together the egg yolks, mustard, cayenne pepper and a pinch of salt. Once the salt has dissolved, gradually whisk in the oil. The sauce should resemble stiff-peaked whipped cream.

3 Squeeze out the excess liquid from the shredded celeriac and mix the celeriac with the sauce. Season with salt and freshly ground black pepper, if necessary. Serve the rémoulade in a large bowl or in small domes on individual plates, decorated with the salad leaves, tomato and walnut halves.

Stuffed cabbage

This is an excellent luncheon or supper dish. In some countries, cabbage is not regarded as a vegetable suitable for serving as a separate course, but the following is definitely worthy of being offered in this way.

Preparation time **45 minutes**
Total cooking time **1 hour 35 minutes**
Serves 6

1 green cabbage, about 500–800 g (1 lb–1 lb 10 oz)
60 g (2 oz) unsalted butter
1 small onion, finely chopped
120 g (4 oz) fresh breadcrumbs
4 tablespoons chopped fresh parsley
1 tablespoon chopped fresh thyme leaves
grated rind of ¹/2 lemon
2 eggs, beaten
15 g (¹/2 oz) clarified butter (see page 63)

1 Trim off any tired cabbage leaves, but leave the cabbage whole. Plunge it into a large pan of boiling water. Boil for 3–4 minutes. Tip off the hot water, transfer the cabbage to a colander and drain well. Allow to cool slightly. Carefully detach four to six outside leaves and set aside. Cut the cabbage into quarters, remove the stalk, then slice the cabbage and chop finely.

2 Melt the butter in a large pan, add the onion, cover and cook gently for 1–2 minutes. Add the cabbage, press a piece of buttered paper on the top, cover the pan and cook over low heat for 25–30 minutes, stirring thoroughly once or twice during cooking. The cabbage should be soft and golden all through. Draw aside, stir in 90 g (3 oz) of the breadcrumbs, the herbs, lemon rind and eggs, and season with salt and pepper.

3 Line a large pudding basin with a buttered piece of muslin or clean cloth. Arrange the reserved outside leaves in this, stalks uppermost. Fill with the mixture, gather the ends of the cloth tightly, twist and tie the cloth to give the cabbage a plump shape. Lift out of the basin, and plunge the cabbage into a pan of boiling salted water or vegetable stock. Boil gently and steadily for 45 minutes to 1 hour. Turn it over once or twice during cooking. Lift out into a colander, drain well, untie the cloth and turn the cabbage over onto a hot dish.

4 Melt the clarified butter in a small pan, add the remaining breadcrumbs and fry until golden. Sprinkle over the cabbage and serve at once with a tomato sauce or well-seasoned passata poured around.

Green beans with bacon

Very popular as a vegetable on the side, served with grilled or baked meats or chicken.
The salty flavour of bacon blends perfectly with green beans.

*Preparation time **10 minutes***
*Total cooking time **15 minutes***
*Serves **4–6***

500 g (1 lb) green beans
1 teaspoon salt
300 g (10 oz) smoked bacon
50 g (1³/4 oz) unsalted butter
3 tablespoons finely chopped fresh parsley

1 Top and tail the beans. Bring a large saucepan of water to the boil. Add the salt and the beans and simmer for 10 minutes, or until tender. Drain and refresh with cold water to stop the cooking process. Drain well.
2 Meanwhile, remove the rind from the bacon and discard. Cut the bacon into small, short strips. Heat a frying pan, add the bacon and fry over medium heat.

There is no need to add any fat, the bacon's own fat will melt into the pan as it cooks. Remove the bacon and drain on paper towels.
3 Drain the excess fat from the pan, wipe with paper towels and then melt the butter in the pan. Toss the beans in the butter, add the bacon and season with salt and pepper. As soon as they are warmed through, transfer to a serving dish, sprinkle with chopped parsley and serve.

Chef's tips To maintain the green colour of the beans, simultaneously throw the salt and the beans into the boiling water. This creates a fast bubble, which helps to fix the chlorophyll.

As a variation, substitute the bacon with two or three tinned anchovy fillets. Prepare them first by soaking in milk, draining and then drying them. Finely chop them and toss in the butter.

Gratin dauphinois

This potato dish has many versions, some with onion or other vegetables added, some with stock and different herbs. Seasoning, cheese, cream and garlic are the key to making this particular version successful. Experiment to suit your own taste.

Preparation time **30 minutes**
Total cooking time **1 hour**
Serves **4–6**

500 g (1 lb) potatoes
500 ml (16 fl oz) milk
nutmeg, grated
100 ml (3¹/4 fl oz) thick (double) cream
1 clove garlic, chopped or minced
100 g (3¹/4 oz) Swiss cheese, grated

1 Preheat the oven to warm 170°C (325°F/Gas 3).
2 Thinly slice the potatoes. Place in a saucepan, cover with the milk and season with some salt, pepper and grated nutmeg.
3 Bring to a simmer over medium-low heat and simmer until the potato is almost cooked but still firm. Strain and set the milk aside.
4 Rub a 20 x 16 cm (8 x 6¹/2 inch) ovenproof dish with some butter. Arrange the potato in even layers in the dish.
5 Reheat the milk and allow to simmer for a few minutes. Add the cream and garlic, bring back to a simmer and check the seasoning. Simmer for a few minutes, then pour over the potato. Sprinkle with the grated cheese and bake for 35–45 minutes, or until the potato is tender and the top is lightly browned.

Chef's tip When making a sauce to accompany a bland vegetable such as potatoes, be sure to season it well.

Vichy carrots

The water used for cooking this dish should really be Vichy water, a natural and healthy mineral water from the springs at Vichy in France. These carrots are a colourful accompaniment to veal and chicken dishes.

*Preparation time **15–20 minutes***
*Total cooking time **20–30 minutes***
Serves 4

600 g (1 1/4 lb) carrots
30 g (1 oz) sugar
60 g (2 oz) unsalted butter
30 g (1 oz) chopped fresh parsley

1 Peel the carrots, slice thinly and put in a pan with enough water to barely cover. Add a pinch of salt as well as the sugar and butter and cover with a paper lid made from a round of greaseproof paper (see Chef's tips).
2 Cook over high heat until almost all the water has evaporated, leaving a syrupy reduction. The carrots should be tender. If not, add a little more water (about

60 ml/2 fl oz) and continue cooking. Toss the carrots to evenly coat them. Sprinkle with the chopped fresh parsley and serve in a deep dish.

Chef's tips The carrots can be cut in different shapes for a more decorative presentation.

A paper lid serves to slow the process of steam escaping, allowing foods to remain moist and prevent them from cooking too quickly. To make a paper lid, prepare a piece of greaseproof paper larger than the diameter of the pan. Fold in half, then in quarters and fold once again into a fan shape. To measure the diameter of the pan, place the point in the centre of the pan and cut at the point the folded paper reaches the edge of the pan. Snip the point and unfold. The paper should now be a circle about the same diameter as the pan with a small hole in the centre.

Braised witlof

*A vegetable that is wonderful braised, even though it is often thought
of as being a salad ingredient.*

*Preparation time **15 minutes***
*Total cooking time **1 hour 30 minutes***
Serves 4

60 g (2 oz) unsalted butter
4 witlof (chicory)
500 ml (16 fl oz) chicken stock
   (see page 63) or water
I tablespoon lemon juice
¹/₂ teaspoon sugar
I teaspoon chopped fresh parsley

1 Preheat the oven to moderate 180°C (350°F/Gas 4).
Grease a baking dish with one third of the butter.
Remove any blemished outer leaves of the witlof and
trim and core the root end. This removes some of the
bitterness. Wash and place them in the prepared dish.

2 Add the chicken stock or water with the lemon juice
to the dish. Season lightly with salt, pepper and the
sugar. Bring to the boil on the stove top. Remove and
cover with buttered greaseproof paper and then foil.
Transfer to the oven and bake for about 1–1¹/4 hours, or
until the witlof are tender. Remove the witlof and place
on a rack to drain, reserving the cooking liquid. Cook
the liquid over high heat until syrupy. Set aside and
keep warm.

3 Once the witlof are cooled, lightly tie in the middle
with some kitchen string. Heat the remaining butter in
a non-stick frying pan and brown the witlof until they
are nicely coloured. Remove the string, place the witlof
in a serving dish and cover with the reduced cooking
liquid. Sprinkle with the parsley.

Chef's tip Before tying with the string, you can wrap a
slice of bacon around the middle.

Grilled marinated vegetables

Served cold with a vinaigrette or hot straight from the grill, these vegetables make a delicious light dish, full of colour and flavour.

Preparation time **20 minutes + 2 hours marinating**
Total cooking time **40 minutes**
Serves 6

1 eggplant (aubergine), about 200 g (6 1/2 oz)
250 g (8 oz) zucchini (courgettes)
200 g (6 1/2 oz) carrots
3 large red capsicums (peppers)
70 g (2 1/4 oz) button mushrooms, washed
2 sprigs of fresh thyme, finely chopped
2 sprigs of fresh parsley, finely chopped
170 ml (5 1/2 fl oz) olive oil
1 tablespoon lemon juice, freshly squeezed
3 tablespoons chopped fresh basil
2 1/2 tablespoons balsamic vinegar

1 Cut the eggplant, zucchini and carrots lengthways into 1 cm (1/2 inch) thick, long slices. Halve the capsicums, remove the seeds and halve into quarters. Remove the mushroom stalks.

2 Spread the vegetables on a tray, sprinkle with salt and pepper, the thyme and parsley. Reserve 2 tablespoons of the olive oil and combine the rest with the lemon juice. Pour over the vegetables and sprinkle with the basil. Marinate for 2 hours.

3 Heat a grill or barbecue and brush with the remaining oil. Slowly grill the vegetables on both sides until tender. (If you prefer less crunchy carrots, grill them for a few minutes before adding the other vegetables.)

4 Arrange the vegetables on a dish and drizzle with the balsamic vinegar.

Vegetable lasagne

Try this deliciously different lasagne with its crunchy vegetables and cheese sauce with a hint of nutmeg. Making your own pasta is both enjoyable and satisfying.

*Preparation time **1 hour + 30 minutes resting***
*Total cooking time **1 hour 30 minutes***
Serves 6

PASTA DOUGH
300 g (10 oz) plain flour
3 eggs, lightly beaten
30 ml (1 fl oz) olive oil
1 teaspoon salt

CHEESE SAUCE
25 g (³/4 oz) unsalted butter
25 g (³/4 oz) plain flour
500 ml (16 fl oz) milk
1/4 teaspoon ground nutmeg
75 ml (2¹/2 fl oz) cream
100 g (3¹/4 oz) Gruyère cheese, grated

25 g (³/4 oz) unsalted butter
1 small onion, sliced
4 ripe tomatoes, peeled, seeded
  and chopped (see page 62)
1 sprig of fresh thyme
1 bay leaf
200 g (6¹/2 oz) carrots, diced
250 g (8 oz) small broccoli florets
1/2 cauliflower, cut into florets
80 g (2³/4 oz) Gruyère cheese, grated

1 To make the pasta, sift the flour onto a work surface and make a large well in the centre in which to place the eggs, olive oil and salt. Using the fingertips of one hand, mix these together and gradually work in the flour until it is all incorporated. The dough should be slightly dry.

Knead until smooth and silky. Kneading will result in the elasticity and texture required, so don't add extra liquid. Wrap in plastic wrap and rest for 20 minutes.

2 To make the cheese sauce, melt the butter in a pan, stir in the flour with a wooden spoon and cook gently for 3 minutes, stirring continuously. Remove from the heat and whisk in the cold milk. Blend thoroughly, season with salt and pepper and add the nutmeg. Return to the heat and bring slowly to the boil, stirring continuously. Lower the heat and cook for 7 minutes, stirring occasionally. Stir in the cream and cheese. Set aside, covered with buttered greaseproof paper.

3 Heat the butter in a pan and cook the onion slowly without browning. Add the tomato, thyme and bay leaf. Season with salt and pepper. Simmer for 15 minutes, or until pulpy. Discard the bay leaf and thyme.

4 Bring a large pan of salted water to the boil. Add the carrot, reduce the heat and simmer for 4 minutes. Add the broccoli and cauliflower and simmer for 3 minutes. Drain and refresh with cold water to stop the cooking process. Drain well and set aside.

5 Preheat the oven to moderately hot 190°C (375°F/ Gas 5). On a lightly floured surface, roll out the pasta dough to 1 mm (1/16 inch) thick. Cut with a sharp knife into long strips 8 x 15 cm (3 x 6 inches) and cook a few strips at a time, in a large pan of boiling salted water with a dash of oil, for 2–3 minutes, or until *al dente*. Transfer to a bowl of cold water, drain and put between layers of tea towel.

6 Mix the cheese and tomato sauces and simmer for 15 minutes. Add the vegetables to the sauce. Season. Butter a 2–2.5-litre capacity ovenproof dish and alternate layers of pasta and vegetable mixture, finishing with pasta. Sprinkle cheese over the top and bake for 35 minutes.

Broccoli purée with blue cheese

Puréed broccoli goes well with almost any dish. Add the cheese only moments before serving.

Preparation time **10 minutes**
Total cooking time **20 minutes**
Serves 4–6

450 g (14¼ oz) broccoli
40 g (1¼ oz) unsalted butter
45 g (1½ oz) blue cheese, grated or finely crumbled

1 Trim the individual broccoli stalks from the main stem, discard the stem and check that about 220 g (7 oz) of broccoli remains. Wash thoroughly and drain, then trim and slice the stalks very thinly, reserving the flower heads.

2 Melt the butter in a medium pan, add the sliced stalks, cover with greaseproof paper and a lid. Cook very gently for 10 minutes until tender, but not coloured. Finely chop the flower heads and add them to the pan with 125 ml (4 fl oz) water. Cook, uncovered, for 5 minutes until tender, but still bright green. Drain well, transfer to a food processor and blend until smooth. Return to the pan, reheat and remove from the heat to stir in the cheese. Season, to taste, with salt and pepper.

3 Serve the purée as oval quenelle shapes by pushing a rounded dessertspoon of purée off the spoon using another spoon, both held horizontally, or simply serve it in a neat mound.

Chef's tip A great accompaniment to meat, fish or poultry, and especially good with steak. Do not add the cheese until just before serving or it may become stringy with overheating.

Carrot purée

For this method of cooking, the carrots should be sliced very thinly so they will cook quickly and evenly.

Preparation time **10 minutes**
Total cooking time **20 minutes**
Serves 4–6

40 g (1¼ oz) unsalted butter
450 g (14¼ oz) carrots, thinly sliced
pinch of nutmeg or ground coriander

1 Melt the butter in a large shallow frying pan, add the carrot and season with salt and pepper. Add the nutmeg or coriander. Cover the pan with a sheet of greaseproof paper and a lid. It is important to cover to prevent loss of steam made by the carrots as they cook, or they will dry and turn brown.

2 Cook over low heat for 15 minutes, or until very soft and tender enough to be mashed with a fork, then remove the paper and lid. Cook, uncovered, over high heat to reduce any excess moisture, then cool slightly. Purée in a food processor until smooth. Return to the pan, adjust the seasoning and reheat to serve. Serve the purée as oval quenelle shapes by pushing a rounded dessertspoon of purée off the spoon using another spoon, both held horizontally, or simply serve it in a neat mound.

Chef's tip The purée may be reheated in the microwave as long as it is in a suitable container.

Carrot purée (top) and Broccoli purée with blue cheese

Warm lentil salad with mustard seed vinaigrette

This traditional regional salad, high in protein, may be served with crustaceans such as prawns. Normally, the small French Puy lentils are used as they hold their shape well. However, other lentils with the same qualities could be substituted for these. Red lentils are not suitable as they soften to a purée.

*Preparation time **15 minutes + overnight soaking***
*Total cooking time **40 minutes***
Serves 6

250 g (8 oz) lentils
50 g (1³/4 oz) unsalted butter
100 g (3¹/4 oz) carrots, diced
¹/2 onion, diced
100 g (3¹/4 oz) smoked bacon, diced
300 ml (10 fl oz) chicken stock (see page 63)
I lettuce

VINAIGRETTE
30 g (I oz) wholegrain mustard
2 teaspoons white wine vinegar
100 ml (3¹/4 fl oz) olive or peanut (groundnut) oil
3 tablespoons chopped fresh parsley

1 Soak the lentils in cold water overnight. Drain.
2 Melt the butter in a large saucepan, add the vegetables and bacon and cook gently until the vegetables are soft, but not brown. Add the lentils and chicken stock to the saucepan. Cover and simmer very gently for 30–35 minutes, or until the lentils are tender. Season with salt and pepper.
3 Pour the mixture into a sieve to drain off the liquid. Transfer the lentils, vegetables and the bacon to a large bowl.
4 To make the vinaigrette, place the mustard and vinegar in a bowl and whisk to combine. Season with salt and freshly ground black pepper and very slowly add the olive or peanut oil, whisking constantly. Finally, add the parsley.
5 Toss the warm lentils, vegetables and bacon with the vinaigrette. Arrange a bed of lettuce leaves on a plate and pile the warm salad in the centre.

Vegetables in white wine

Experiment with different vegetables to see which you prefer. Make this dish according to the traditional recipe below, or vary it with an oriental touch or your favourite herbs.

*Preparation time **1 hour***
*Total cooking time **50 minutes***
*Serves **4***

2 tablespoons olive oil
100 g (3¼ oz) bacon, cut into strips
3 French shallots, finely chopped
1 large carrot, cut into batons (see page 63)
1 celery stick, cut into batons
½ fennel root, cut into batons
100 ml (3¼ fl oz) white wine
100 ml (3¼ fl oz) chicken stock (see page 63)
  or water
2 large tomatoes, peeled, seeded
  and diced (see page 62)
100 g (3¼ oz) shelled fresh peas
100 g (3¼ oz) French beans,
  topped and tailed
60 g (2 oz) toasted pine nuts

1 In a large frying pan, heat the oil over medium heat and cook the bacon until golden brown. Lower the heat, add the shallots and a pinch of salt. Cook for 2 minutes, without colouring. Add the carrot, celery, fennel and a pinch of salt, and cook gently for 5 minutes.

2 Add the white wine and chicken stock and cook over medium heat until almost dry. Add the tomato and cook for 5–10 minutes, or until tender.

3 In two separate saucepans, cook the peas and French beans in boiling salted water for 8–10 minutes, or until tender. Drain and refresh in iced water until completely cooled. Drain well and add to the other vegetables. Leave to simmer for 3–5 minutes, or until hot, and season with salt and pepper, to taste. Just before serving, sprinkle with toasted pine nuts. Serve hot or cold.

Chef's tip Slow cooking is a must when preparing this dish, in order to keep it moist. For a more oriental flavour, add toasted sesame seeds instead of the pine nuts and use a little soy sauce instead of salt.

Chef's techniques

◆

Preparing tomatoes

Many recipes call for peeled, seeded tomatoes. It is an easy process if you follow these instructions.

Using a very sharp knife, score a small cross in the base of each tomato.

Blanch the tomatoes in a large pan of boiling water for 10 seconds. Remove and plunge into a bowl of ice cold water to stop the cooking and keep the flesh firm.

Pull away the skin from the cross, and discard the skins.

If a recipe calls for the removal of the tomato seeds, cut the tomato in half and use a teaspoon to gently scoop out the seeds.

Preparing whole artichokes

You can cook either the whole artichoke, as shown below, or just the heart. Both are delicious.

Break off the artichoke stalk at the bottom, pulling out the fibres that attach it to the base.

Pull off the outer leaves and place the artichoke in a pan of boiling salted water with the juice of 1 lemon. Weigh down with a plate and simmer for 20–35 minutes.

Test for doneness by pulling at one of the leaves. If it comes away easily, the artichoke is done. Cut off the top half of the artichoke and discard.

Remove the hairy choke in the middle of the artichoke with a spoon. The artichoke bottom is now ready to fill.

Clarifying butter

Removing the water and solids from butter makes it less likely to burn. Ghee is a form of clarified butter.

To make 100 g (3¹/4 oz) clarified butter, cut 180 g (5³/4 oz) butter into small cubes. Place in a small pan set into a larger pot of water over low heat. Melt the butter, without stirring.

Remove the pan from the heat and allow to cool slightly. Skim the foam from the surface, being careful not to stir the butter.

Pour off the clear yellow liquid, being very careful to leave the milky sediment behind in the pan. Discard the sediment and store the clarified butter in an airtight container in the refrigerator.

Making chicken stock

Good, flavoursome home-made stock can be the cornerstone of a great dish.

Cut up 750 g (1¹/2 lb) chicken bones and carcass and put in a pan with a roughly chopped onion, carrot and celery stick. Add 6 peppercorns, a bouquet garni and 4 litres cold water.

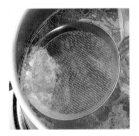

Bring to the boil and let the stock simmer gently for 2–3 hours, skimming off any scum that rises to the surface using a large spoon. Strain the stock through a sieve into a clean bowl, then allow to cool.

Chill the stock overnight, then lift off any fat. If you can't leave overnight, drag the surface of the hot strained stock with paper towels to lift off the fat. Makes 1.5–2 litres.

Baton vegetables

Evenly sized vegetables cook uniformly and look attractive in dishes such as ratatouille.

Use a long, very sharp knife to cut the vegetables into batons.

Washing leeks

Leeks are often used in cooking as they impart a unique flavour.

Before use, leeks need to be rinsed thoroughly under cold running water to dislodge and remove all traces of dirt or grit. Slit the green tops to help the water run through the tightly furled leaves.

Published by Murdoch Books® a division of Murdoch Magazines Pty Limited, 213 Miller Street, North Sydney NSW 2060.

Murdoch Books and Le Cordon Bleu thank the 32 masterchefs of all the Le Cordon Bleu Schools, whose knowledge and expertise have made this book possible, especially: Chef Cliche (MOF), Chef Terrien, Chef Boucheret, Chef Duchêne (MOF), Chef Guillut, Chef Steneck, Paris; Chef Males, Chef Walsh, Chef Hardy, London; Chef Chantefort, Chef Bertin, Chef Jambert, Chef Honda, Tokyo; Chef Salembien, Chef Boutin, Chef Harris, Sydney; Chef Lawes, Adelaide; Chef Guiet, Chef Denis, Ottawa. Of the many students who helped the Chefs test each recipe, a special mention to graduates David Welch and Allen Wertheim. A very special acknowledgment to Directors Susan Eckstein, Great Britain, and Kathy Shaw, Paris, who have been responsible for the coordination of the Le Cordon Bleu team throughout this series.

Murdoch Books®
Managing Editor: Kay Halsey
Series Concept, Design and Art Direction: Juliet Cohen
Editor: Wendy Stephen
Food Director: Jody Vassallo
Food Editors: Lulu Grimes, Tracy Rutherford
Designer: Marylouise Brammer
Photographers: Joe Filshie, Chris Jones
Food Stylists: Carolyn Fienberg, Mary Harris
Food Preparation: Jo Forrest, Kerrie Ray
Chef's Techniques Photographer: Reg Morrison
Home Economists: Michelle Lawton, Kerrie Mullins, Justine Poole, Kerrie Ray

CEO & Publisher: Anne Wilson
Publishing Director: Catie Ziller
General Manager: Mark Smith
Creative Director: Marylouise Brammer
International Sales Director: Mark Newman

National Library of Australia Cataloguing-in-Publication Data
Vegetables. ISBN 0 86411 734 5. 1. Cookery (Vegetables). (Series: Le Cordon Bleu home collection). 641.65

Printed by Toppan Printing (S) Pte Ltd
First Printed 1997
©Design and photography Murdoch Books® 1997
©Text Le Cordon Bleu 1997
Distributed in the UK by D Services, 6 Euston Street, Freemen's Common, Leicester LE2 7SS Tel 0116-254-7671 Fax 0116-254-4670. Distributed in Canada by Whitecap (Vancouver) Ltd, 351 Lynn Avenue, North Vancouver, BC V7J 2C4 Tel 604-980-9852 Fax 604-980-8197 or Whitecap (Ontario) Ltd, 47 Coldwater Road, North York, ON M3B 1Y8 Tel 416-444-3442 Fax 416-444-6630

The Publisher and Le Cordon Bleu wish to thank Carole Sweetnam for her help with this series.
Front cover, from top: Provençal stuffed tomatoes; Mixed glazed vegetables; Green beans with bacon.

IMPORTANT INFORMATION

CONVERSION GUIDE

1 cup = 250 ml (8 fl oz)
1 Australian tablespoon = 20 ml (4 teaspoons)
1 UK tablespoon = 15 ml (3 teaspoons)

NOTE: We have used 20 ml tablespoons. If you are using a 15 ml tablespoon, for most recipes the difference will be negligible. For recipes using baking powder, gelatine, bicarbonate of soda and flour, add an extra teaspoon for each tablespoon specified.

CUP CONVERSIONS—DRY INGREDIENTS

1 cup flour, plain or self-raising = 125 g (4 oz)
1 cup sugar, caster = 250 g (8 oz)
1 cup breadcrumbs, dry = 125 g (4 oz)

IMPORTANT: Those who might be at risk from the effects of salmonella food poisoning (the elderly, pregnant women, young children and those suffering from immune deficiency diseases) should consult their GP with any concerns about eating raw eggs.